BLACK
HISTORY
ACCORDING TO
GOD'S WORD

HENRY L. RAZOR

S.H.E. PUBLISHING, LLC

Black History According To God's Word

Copyright © 2024 by Henry L. Razor

For information contact: www.shepublishingllc.com

Library of Congress Control Number: 2023952264

ISBN:
978-1-953163-89-9 (hardback)
978-1-953163-88-2 (paperback)

First Edition: January 2024

10 9 8 7 6 5 4 3 2 1

DEDICATION

This book is dedicated to the many enlightened individuals
who labor for the truth of God's word to be spread abroad
upon the face of this earth.

TABLE *of* CONTENTS

PREFACE

When writing any book that discusses history or historical topics, it is important that the information presented be researched, sourced, and above all accurate. This task becomes even more important when the history that is being written about is the history of man. And to add even more complexity to the topic, this history of man will discuss ethnic origins, the beginnings of nations, and will marry the scriptural account of man's beginning with the science that validates and authenticates the scripture. And as complex as it may appear to be, the Biblically Black and Blessed series of books does just that.

With this book, the third in the series, I have created a book that can be used as a teaching aid in schools, Sunday Schools, Bible classes, seminars, conferences, etc. This book is purposed for Black History like none other. And it is this author's position that Black History should be taught all year long because it is the history of mankind. Without dismissing, denigrating, or attacking others, I will present the entire history of Black People in a chronological order beginning with the first man. This will be done using the Holy Scriptures as the primary source of information, with science and other external sources validating and verifying scripture. It has taken decades of prayer, study, and research to accumulate this information, and present it with the rightly divided word of truth.

Many myths are dispelled. Incorrect teachings and arguments are corrected. I am sure that you will learn so much more about the people of African heritage and our relationship with the Creator. And, as with the previous books in this series, every chunk of data and every bit of information is supported with scripture and sourced with credible sources on the topic. And I must also say that much of the foundational information appears in the previous two books of this series, so I will not re-produce this information. When necessary, I will reference the points from the previous books, and at times the information in this book will build on the information provided in the previous books. And when this occurs, I will reference the book and section from the previous books where you can locate the information; but time and space prevents me from re-creating this information within the pages of this book. Although the previous books in this series are referenced and the information from those books is built upon, this book is a stand-a-lone book to be used for teaching Black History that occurred prior to 1619.

Oh, and one last thing before moving on from this preface. **THIS BOOK IS NOT INTENDED TO EXALT ANY GROUP OF PEOPLE ABOVE ANOTHER!** It does not espouse the idea that any one group of people is superior to another, nor does it promote the idea that any one group of people has attained a greater degree of favorability with God. This book merely takes the word of God as written, applies research from credible sources, and then presents the history of mankind, highlighting Black People because they are the focus of this project. As a Black male that was raised in the Bible belt, church was an integral part of my life. But in all of my years of attending church from my youth to becoming a young adult, only once did I witness a minister deliver a sermon on the people of African heritage. That one time had such an impact on my life that it motivated me to know more. (*I mention this time in the introduction of this book.*) I heard messages on the descendents of Noah's son Shem (Jewish People and Arabs)[1]; I heard messages on the descendents of

---

[1] Genesis 10:21-31

ii

Noah's son Japheth (Gentiles)[2]; but never heard I messages on the descendents of Noah's son Ham (the Children of The Ethiopians and all Indigenous Africans).[3] As I commenced studying, praying, searching the scriptures, and researching, I discovered that the descendents of Noah's son Ham were instrumental in the creation of humanity and were in relationship with God so closely that they became the standard for how God related to the Jewish people.[4] Possessing the biblical knowledge of the descendents of Ham while hardly, if ever, hearing preachers deliver messages or teach about them left me perplexed. How could people who are so prominent in God's orchestrated plan for humanity and enjoy such an impenetrable relationship with God be so overlooked or dismissed while ministering the scriptures? This book will provide answers to this question and many more while presenting the history of Black People and highlighting our highly regarded and precious relationship with God.

---

[2] Genesis 10:2-5
[3] Genesis 10:6-20
[4] Amos 9:7

FOREWORD

When asked by the author to write the forward for this book, I was elated. Why? Because of my profound respect for him. As a sophomore in high school, I found myself struggling with Algebra I. I remember a young, astute, and confident Henry Razor sitting with me at my parents' (Finus and Lizzie Jones) kitchen table in Earle, Arkansas I shared with him that I feared that I was going to make my first failing grade. He asked which subject I was struggling with. I responded that it was Algebra I, and I showed him what I was working on. Now, I believe that my teacher at the time was the consummate professional and a great educator who cared about her students and wanted us all to succeed. I really liked her. However, regardless of her best efforts, I could not grasp what she was attempting to instill in me. Then came my friend Henry, who was two grades ahead of me, asking if I wanted him to help me. Of course, I desperately replied, "yes". He then took one of the most complex algebraic equations and showed me how to break it down, then work through it, Henry, explained in detail each step and why it was important in solving the problem. He explained it all to me in the most simplistic and understandable manner. Then, he challenged me to give it a try on my own. Light Bulb! Henry then watched me solve equation after equation until he was confident in my confidence level. Then we ate one of Mom's delicious meals. I'm happy to share that I not only passed the class, but I received a high "B" in it. I went on to do well in Algebra II and Trigonometry before graduating from high school. After struggling in the beginning with Algebra, I vowed to never take another advanced math class, but I credit Razor with opening my eyes to how to navigate through complex equations and reinforcing my confidence in my ability to do the work.

In **Black History According to God's Word**, my friend, Pastor Henry L. Razor, does it again. From the first page, I couldn't stop reading, as he takes another complicated topic, the origin of man, and dissects it in this simple, yet insightful book. He not only debunks some of the myths that have been around for centuries, he also proves his conclusions with carefully source research and illustrations. In this book he shares how his humble beginning in our beloved Earle, Arkansas stoked his thirst for more knowledge around the origin of our existence. Razor's years of research and travels around the globe have informed his work and his conclusions.

This book made me feel 10 feet taller with pride as a Black man while not diminishing any other race of people. Expertly illustrated with relevant timelines and maps, it is a must read if you are interested in the true origin of our Black ancestry. Throughout each of our lives, we have often heard opinions and generalities of our origin. Usually, this was never backed up with evidence or facts, and often false. This prolific writer opens your mind to our journey from Adam and Eve to Noah and his sons, to the seeds of Abraham and beyond. Razor reveals the impact of Black people on the invention of writing, to the forming of the first school libraries, to the formation of the first government, pharmacy, and impact on agriculture just to name a few.

So take the words of this writer, verify the conclusions for yourself then share them with others. I am in awe with what the pages of this book reveal. I believe that you will be too.

Steven B. Jones, Member of the Arkansas House of
Representatives (1999-2005)

BLACK HISTORY

HISTORY

ACCORDING TO
GOD'S WORD

HENRY L. RAZOR

INTRODUCTION

This is the third book in the 'Biblically Black and Blessed' series of books that I have written. Although not directly titled 'Biblically Black and Blessed' as the previous books are, this book represents a pulling together of data, facts, history, and research that will empower the message of the previous two books and serve as a reference and teaching aid for generations of youth to come. Every Believer, especially Believers of African ancestry, should have this book in their library.

For a portion of my youth, Black History Month was not in existence, being an African American growing up in the Mississippi Delta region of the United States. When February was officially designated as the month to recognize the contributions that people of African ancestry have made to the world, it was hardly, if ever, celebrated in the portion of the south where I lived during my youth. I have no memory of Black History acknowledgements or celebrations from my schooling, my church, or even within my family. Except for a few TV movies about Dr. Martin Luther King Jr. and a few other TV specials that highlighted those that fought for equality, I grew from early childhood into adulthood without acknowledging and recognizing the history making contributions to this world of so many people of African ancestry. It was as if Dr. Martin Luther King Jr. was the only person of African Ancestry that contributed to society. So in my earliest of years, Dr Martin Luther King Jr. was Black History. There were pictures of him with John and Robert Kennedy hanging in our house. If ever I enquired about the plight of black people, I would be provided with a response that always included Dr. Martin Luther King Jr. As I grew older, it became apparent to me that if I wanted to know my history, I would have to set out on a journey and acquire this knowledge for myself. And this I did.

As a young adult I started seriously researching the history of my people. And all of the data that I was able to obtain always took me back to a day in Virginia, in the year 1619. And as I started learning about black people from that time to the present, I was thrilled to learn of the inventors, philosophers, activists, and other great people of African ancestry. But even knowing this there seemed to be something missing. How could it be that our history started in 1619? Where were our ancestors prior to 1619? What was life like for our ancestors prior to being forced into chattel slavery? These questions and many more kept nagging at me and pushing me to seek more information, to dig deeper for understanding, and work harder for true knowledge.

I grew into adulthood as a member of the Church of God In Christ. Our congregation located in Earle, Arkansas was a vibrant community of believers that loved God, loved fellowship, and loved each other. We were in the heart of the Mississippi Delta and because times were hard, we were more like a big family. And because many of us never really had a vacation, the leaders of our local church would do all that they could do to take us to the local, state, regional, and national church conventions. As a young child and throughout my teen years, these church get-a-ways were the only times that I had ever been away from home, sleeping in a hotel room, and eating from restaurants. These conventions and convocations were the greatest things to me and for me. I looked forward to these meetings and I would save every penny that I could so that I'd have money in my pocket when I attended.

It was in one of our state youth conventions that the fire to know more about my ancestors was initially ignited. The year was 1977, maybe 1978 and I was about 15 years old. We were in Pine Bluff Arkansas at our Annual State Youth Convention. These meetings usually lasted an entire week with locals and those in close proximity attending during the week, but most of the people arrived on Friday because they worked during the week. We were about two hours away so we would get there Friday and stay through Sunday, returning home on Sunday night. As was customary, the State Prelate, the highest church official in the state, would deliver the official message on Sunday afternoon. For our state, this official was Bishop L.T. Walker. Bishop Walker was a preacher's preacher, and he was a very learned man! But what I loved more about him was how he so thoroughly presented the word with facts, resources, and verifiable sources. On this particular Sunday, he delivered a message that included Noah and his three sons. Bishop Walker meticulously laid the foundation for the nations of the world. He spoke of Shem and the Jews, Japheth and the Gentiles, and Ham and the Africans. He dwelled on Ham for a lengthy portion of his message. Maybe it was because our youth conventions were in early March and coming out of February, he wanted to emphasize the newly dedicated Black History Month. Or maybe he wanted to plant a seed of Black History pride in the hearts and minds of so many young black boys and girls in attendance at this convention. Whatever his goal was, he hit a home run with me. He talked about Noah giving birth to Ham, then Ham giving birth to Cush, and Cush's offspring migrating throughout Sub-Saharan Africa. He explained how, as Cush's offspring settled in hot areas that were closer to the equator, their anatomy changed to ensure survival in these climates. He talked about how their hair cells changed to produce hair that was in his words "kanky or nappy" to shield them from the sun; he talked about how their skin darkened to provide inherent resistance to the ultraviolet waves emanating from the sun. He talked about the muscular physique that strengthened them for hunting, water events on the Nile

3

River, and surviving in such a climate. I sat in my seat listening to him as if I was in a trance. I was completely mesmerized! My curiosity had been ignited and I needed to know more. Who was this Ham? And what about Cush? How is Cush my ancestor? How is this lineage my lineage? That was the day that I started my journey to obtain the Bible history of people of African heritage.

One can see how perplexing it was to hear Bishop Walker speak of a Biblical Black lineage, while all of the Black History being presented elsewhere in my world only went back to the first Africans that were brought here as slaves in 1619. This forced me to apply myself more, read more, search more, and research more to get the complete story. The more I researched, the more I learned. The more I learned, the more I became enlightened. The more I became enlightened, the more I realized that what I was seeking HAD BEEN AT MY FINGERTIPS ALL ALONG!

I started searching for descendents of Ham throughout the Bible. What I found was so eye opening that I wrote my first book, **Biblically Black and Blessed – What The Bible Says About God's Relationship With Black People,** about my findings. This book was foundational and a huge success as it brought to light the many indigenous Africans that are written into the Holy Scriptures. In this book I geographically located Eden in Africa using the Holy Scriptures and scientific research. Then I went further to show that both Adam and Eve were Africans, and that indigenous Africans and people of African ancestry have always been close to God, and have always enjoyed a very strong and secure relationship with our creator. I showed that Black People are God's people also, only with a different kingdom assignment than the Jews. At no time did I dismiss the Jewish people as the people that God selected to be the

Priests of the earth[5], but I emphasized they are not God's ONLY people. Truly, if it's God's purpose to establish His kingdom on earth as it is in heaven, then God has different assignments for different people in His kingdom. Everyone is purposed with an assignment within His kingdom, so the other nations too must have divine assignments. In other words, there will be more nations in His kingdom than just the Jews. I closed that book by presenting short informational biographies on many of the Africans mentioned in the Bible.

This detail and information lead me to write the second book in the series. **Biblically Black and Blesses II – The Children of the Ethiopians.** With this book I look at the lineage of the Noah's great grandson Cush. The offspring of Cush is responsible for settling and populating the vast majority of Africa (Sub-Saharan Africa). These people are known throughout the Bible as the "Ethiopians" or the "Children of The Ethiopians". Scripture can be demonstrated that shows that the Ethiopians have always been close to God, have always responded when God called, and served as the example of how God would relate to Israel.[6] We explain that three groups of prominence should be mentioned when discussing the offspring of Noah's three sons. Shem produced the Jews. Japheth produced the Gentiles. Ham produced the Ethiopians. But the most impressive and eye-opening fact about this book is the revealing of the kingdom assignment given to the Ethiopians.

Both of the previous books in the Biblically Black and Blessed series are filled with scriptural knowledge that is the result of years of prayer, study, and research. But as I travel and present on the topics in these books, I am always asked

---

[5] Exodus 19:6
[6] Amos 9:7

this question; "Will you create a class for this and teach our people?" What I've learned is that the majority of people that I encounter would like a book that is understandable at all levels; a book that they can teach from; a book that they can reference quickly; a book that has clear objectives at every level; a book that can be used as a tool, not only during Black History Month, but throughout the year; and more than anything else, a book that is biblically and historically accurate, with scripture support. Reliable, verifiable, and validated sources are also necessary if this book is to be used to teach others. Providing this data within the guidelines just mentioned is the objective of this book.

As I dedicated myself to the quest of learning the history of black people, I soon learned that much of this history was in my hands throughout my life. For the one thing that was consistently used as a guide throughout my life was the Bible. And I learned that within the pages of the Bible is the entire history of black people, FROM THE VERY BEGINNING! As God enlightened me with understanding, I begin to see how Black People, or people of African ancestry, have always been aligned with God and have always been willing and available to God when he called.

So as I begin to disseminate the information that I have acquired and compiled with much prayer, research, and study through the years, I pray that this knowledge enlightens you as it did me; and that with this book you become a more knowledgeable believer in the faith. This book is not only for Black People or people of African Ancestry, but the goal of this book is to enlighten all believers. For with the correct knowledge, we can better understand God's plan for all of humanity and prepare ourselves for the day when the answer to the prayer that Jesus instructed us to pray; "Your kingdom come. Your will be done, on earth as it is in heaven."[7] becomes the reality of our existence.

I pray that this book becomes a valuable resource in your library of life, and that the information within its pages prove to be trustworthy sources in your quest for accurate knowledge. I also pray that this book is used as a biblical and historical document that presents the verifiable facts about the history of Black People; history that is documented both historically, and within the Bible.

---

[7] Matthew 6:10

A BLACK Beginning

7. Then the Lord God formed man of dust from the ground, and breathed into his nostrils the breath of life; and man became a living being.
8. The Lord God planted a garden toward the east, in Eden; and there He placed the man whom He had formed.

Genesis 2:7-8

Any discourse or document professing to provide accurate history should itself reference back to the earliest point possible and there begin by defining the origin of the subject, then proceed from this earliest point of origin with documented, verifiable, and validated data. This means that we will start at the earliest point documented in the Holy Scriptures. I will begin at the point in history where people first existed; I will begin with the creation of man. And from this point in history, I will show how black people came forth as the very first people. To do this, I will create a timeline that will be constantly updated with historical points relative to Black People. This timeline will be a working document within this book.

NOTE: The dates applied to this timeline are derived from biblical genealogical tables, sourced historical data, and sourced scientific documentation. Therefore, the dates are approximate and as precise and exacting as the available sources. The first point to be applied to the timeline will be the creation of Adam and Eve.

Biblical/Historical Timeline

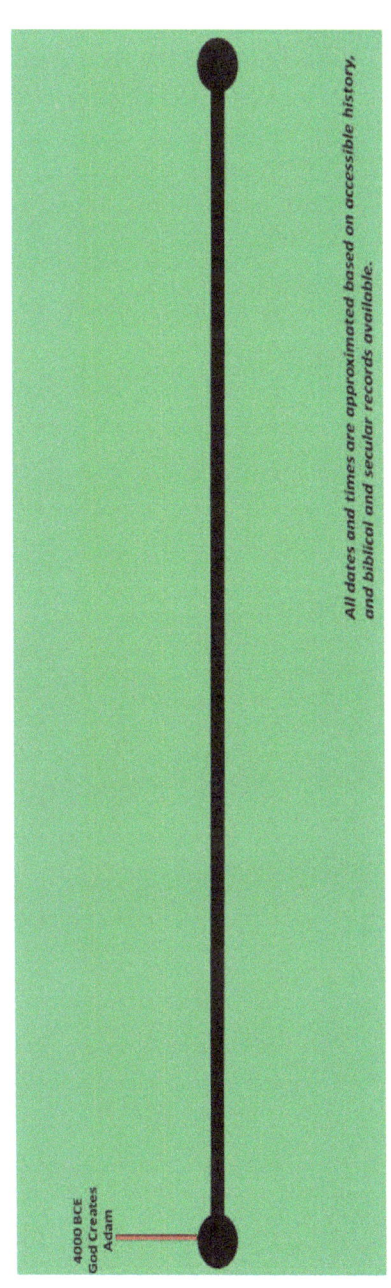

4000 BCE
God Creates Adam

All dates and times are approximated based on accessible history, and biblical and secular records available.

In my first book, **Biblically Black and Blessed- What The Bible Says About God's Relationship With Black People**, I meticulously and accurately locate Eden in Northeast Africa using scripture and scientific sources applied together. The location of Eden will prove to be critical knowledge later as we see the journeying and migratory paths of the earliest people. So if you do not have **Biblically Black and Blessed - What The Bible Says About God's Relationship With Black People**, now is a good time to obtain it and read the chapter titled "*In The Very Beginning*". I also use scripture to show how the pre-Adamic period applies, relative to the beginning of man. The date of Adam's creation was arrived at by using genealogical tables and working backwards from a date that we confidently know.

Location of Eden using scripture & Dr. Cann's research
(*Map taken from Biblically Black and Blessed*)

We arrive at a creation date for Adam by following the biblical genealogical tables of Genesis chapters 5 and chapter 11, then working back from Abraham. With each entry into the table, scripture gives us a length of life, making it possible to work backwards from Abraham with accuracy. Archeological evidence exists that gives us the approximate date of Abraham's birth, so he is the perfect person to center this table around.

Such a table was first produced by 17th-century historian, Archbishop James Ussher, and even though many others have produced like or similar tables, most of them align with Ussher, so I will credit him in the pages of this book for his work.

The following table provides a visual layout of Archbishop's Ussher's work. It was produced by Robert Rouse for Viz Bible. I am using this table with permission of Robert Rouse and Viz Bible.

I created a similar table, but my table only charted the approximate date of birth for each individual in this table. Mr. Rouse's table visually takes the biblical genealogies and tables of nations and gives us time detail that allows us to calculate dates that are both pertinent and relative to our objective.

Genesis Timeline from Adam to Abraham

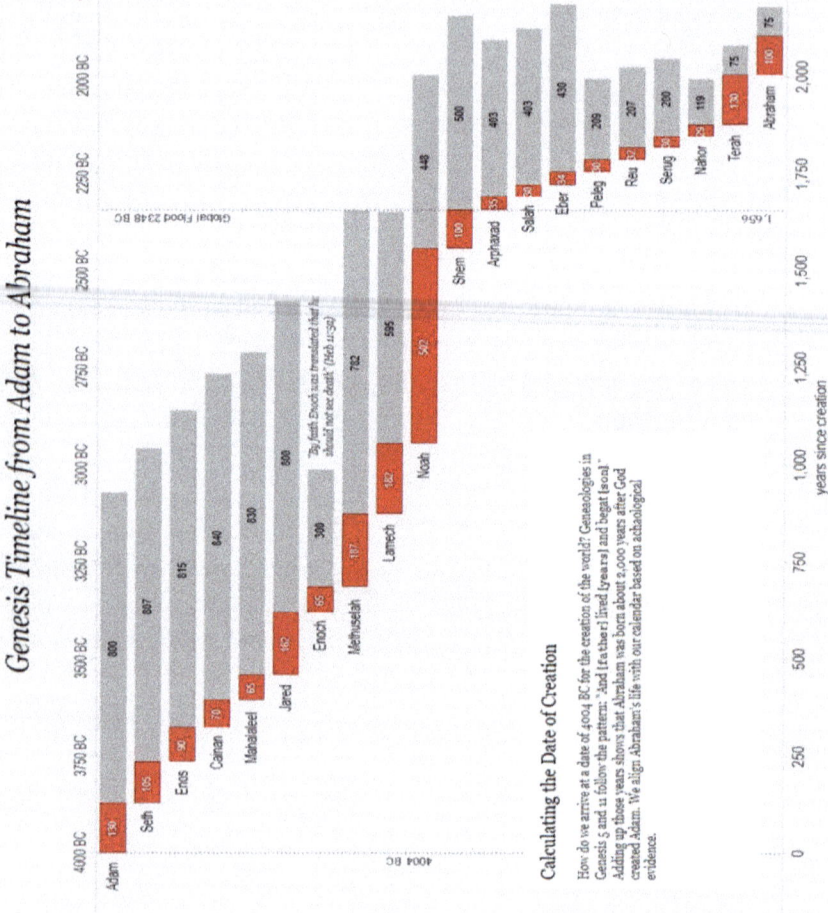

Calculating the Date of Creation

How do we arrive at a date of 4004 BC for the creation of the world? Genealogies in Genesis 5 and 11 follow the pattern: "And [father] lived [years] and begat [son]." Adding up those years shows that Abraham was born about 2,000 years after God created Adam. We align Abraham's life with our calendar based on archeological evidence.

I introduce this 'Genesis Timeline' in table format at this point for two reasons. It is important for you to know how the date of creation for Adam was obtained. But more importantly, this table provides the foundation for most of the dates that will appear throughout this book. I will not repeat this table, but rather I will look back at it in the next chapter for time and date ranges.

My Biblical/Historical Timeline will be repeated multiple times as we encounter people, places, and events that the Bible calls out as pertinent and World History substantiates as relevant. This timeline will serve as a living document within the book and it will chronologically show the people of African heritage at work within God's plan. And as we progress through the Scriptural events and connect them with the historical time period, you will begin to see just how important of a role Black People were assigned in the commencement of humanity and are assigned in the establishment of God's kingdom on earth.

Once we have approximated the time of Adam's creation, the very next logical step is to determine the location of his creation.

The location of Eden is necessary when beginning any discourse on the first humans because this location will provide the relevant information about the humans. This is the primary reason that I took the time and provided the scriptures and sources that established and validated this location in my book **Biblically Black and Blessed - What The Bible Says About God's Relationship With Black People.** Since scripture and applied science locate Eden in Northeast Africa, we can use what we know from that book and confidently confirm that the first man and woman (Adam and Eve) were Africans. Here are five facts that we know about Adam and Eve from scripture.

15

1. Adam was created by God on the sixth day of creation

Genesis 1:26-31

26. Then God said, "Let Us make man in Our image, according to Our likeness; and let them rule over the fish of the sea and over the birds of the sky and over the cattle and over all the earth, and over every creeping thing that creeps on the earth."

27. God created man in His own image, in the image of God He created him; male and female He created them.

28. God blessed them; and God said to them, "Be fruitful and multiply, and fill the earth, and subdue it; and rule over the fish of the sea and over the birds of the sky and over every living thing that moves on the earth."

29. Then God said, "Behold, I have given you every plant yielding seed that is on the surface of all the earth, and every tree which has fruit yielding seed; it shall be food for you;

30. and to every beast of the earth and to every bird of the sky and to every thing that moves on the earth which has life, I have given every green plant for food"; and it was so.

31. God saw all that He had made, and behold, it was very good. And there was evening and there was morning, the sixth day.

2. Adam was created from the ground at the place of creation

Genesis 2:7

7. Then the Lord God formed man of dust from the ground, and breathed into his nostrils the breath of life; and man became a living being.

3. God planted a garden at the place of man's creation

Genesis 2:8
8. The Lord God planted a garden toward the east, in Eden; and there He placed the man whom He had formed.

4. This garden became the residence of man
This fact is validated by the scripture that is used to validate fact number three

5. This garden was located in eastern Eden
Once again, this fact is validated by the scripture used to validate fact number three.

So with the knowledge that Eden was located in northeast Africa, we know that on the sixth day God took African soil and created the first man. Furthermore, we also know that God planted a garden there and placed the first man there. So Africa is the indigenous homeland of the very first man. This would mean that the very first humans were people of African ethnic origin. *Both the Bible and scientific evidence and research validate this fact!*

Humanity indeed was black in the beginning.
For more detailed information on the biblical scriptures and the scientific research used by this author to locate Eden, it is covered in detail in the first chapter of **"Biblically Black and Blessed - What the Bible Says About God's Relationship With Black People."**

WHEN *the* WORLD WAS BLACK

Now the whole earth used the same
language and the same words.
Genesis 11:1

In chapter one, we showed that God placed Eden in Northeast Africa, and Adam was created from the dust of Africa. Therefore, both Adam and Eve were Africans, or they were black. We also know from scriptures that God evicted Adam and Eve from the east side of Eden[8]. Let's take another look at the graphic of Eden within Africa, because this eastern eviction from Eden will prove critical as we progress.

---

[8] Genesis 3:24

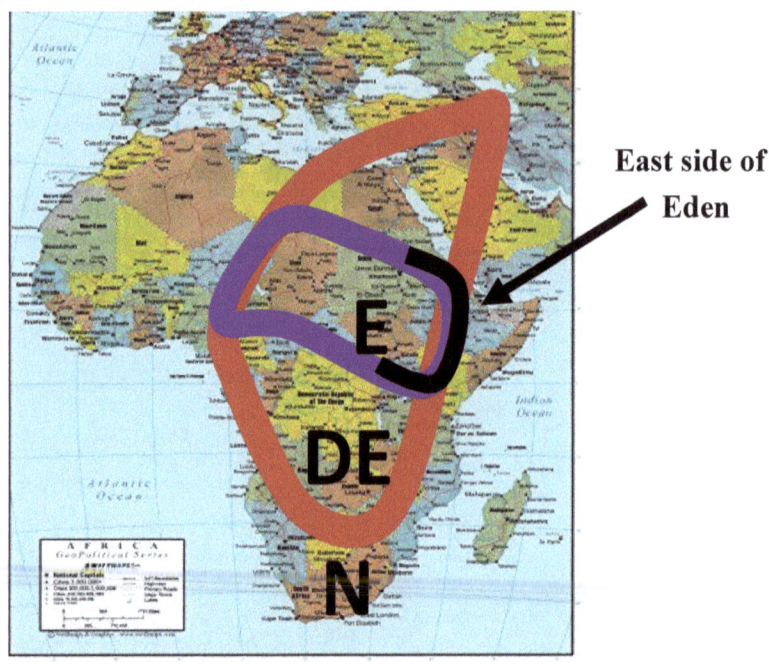

East side of Eden

Shortly after their eviction from Eden, Adam and Eve begin to procreate and replenish the earth. The Bible almost immediately introduces their first two children, Cain and Abel. Everyone that has ever been associated with a church or any ethical or religious institution has heard the story of Cain and Abel. The crux of this story is that the very first murder occurred when Cain, in a jealous rage, slew his brother Abel. And when God questioned him about the whereabouts of his brother, he responded nonchalantly, "I do not know, am I my brother's keeper?"[9] God was angry that Cain had slain his brother, but He became even angrier at

---

[9] Genesis 4:9

Cain's response to His questioning of his brother's whereabouts. God pronounced punishment upon Cain for his insidious act of violence, and Cain departed from the presence of God. But it is interesting to note that God inspired the writers of scripture to include the direction that Cain journeyed at this point. God wanted us to know that Cain travelled East of Eden and settled in the "Land of Nod."[10]

> *"Then Cain went out from the presence of the Lord,*
> *and settled in the land of Nod, east of Eden."*
> **Genesis 4:16**

By providing us with the reference point of Eden, it becomes obvious that the Land of Nod was also on the African continent, slightly east of Eden. We also see a pattern forming here with the first people that we should note. A pattern that, when viewed in light of creation, reveals the beginnings of God's plan to locate the earth's inhabitants in preparation for the establishment of His kingdom on earth. So just what is this pattern?

First, when Adam and Eve messed up in the Garden, they were evicted on the East side of Eden.

Secondly, when Cain messed up and was evicted from the presence of God, he continued the movement of man in an eastern direction. This eastern movement of man in the

---

[10] Genesis 4:16

earliest of days reveals the plan of God for replenishing the earth and expanding His kingdom here. This will become even more obvious as the eastern movement of man becomes the catalyst for life as we know it today. And keep in mind that we are still talking about people on the continent of Africa, yes, these are black people! We see by Cain's response to his punishment that the population of the earth is continually increasing. He is concerned that revenge will be enacted upon him by those who would later learn that he was responsible for Abel's death.

> *"13. Cain said to the Lord, "My punishment is too great to bear!*
> *14. Behold, You have driven me this day from the face of the ground; and from Your face I will be hidden, and I will be a vagrant and a wanderer on the earth, and whoever finds me will kill me."*
>
> **Genesis 4:13-14**

We also know from scripture that Adam and Even had additional sons and daughters.[11] Thus it appears that Cain's concern was that any of the generations of Adam's other sons and daughters would enact this revenge. The population on the earth was booming[12], and just as quickly as it grew, it became corrupted by Satan. God, being grieved by the

---

[11] Genesis 5:4
[12] Genesis 6:1

constant and continual evilness of man, decided to destroy everyone and everything that He had created and re-start the replenishment of the earth with Noah[13]. And God caused the earth to flood by sending rain for forty days and forty nights. But He preserved humanity by saving Noah, his wife, and their three sons with their wives. It would be with Noah's three sons that the earth would be repopulated.[14]Therefore, it is a good time now to provide a concise introduction of Noah's three sons and their succeeding descendents. This will be covered concisely here, as it is thoroughly covered with meticulous detail in the book **"Biblically Black and Blessed - What The Bible Says About God's Relationship With Black People."**

Noah had three sons from which every person on earth today came from.

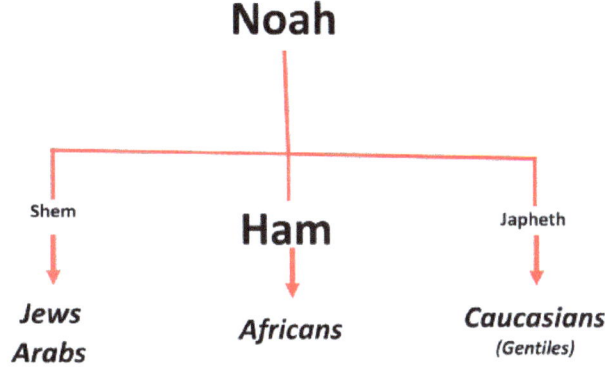

I cannot over emphasize that Noah and his three sons were Africans that resided on the continent somewhere east of Eden. *We will see this a little later as the expanding population journeyed away from Africa.* At this point, there are no ethnicities, no races, no nations, all the people are one. I will at this time place another entry onto my timeline. This point will represent the approximate time when Noah's three sons began repopulating the earth.

At about 2350 BCE, Noah's sons begin to re-populate the earth.

I must emphasize that the Bible does NOT speak of races. God only mentions nations, genealogies, and ethnic origins. Hence, Noah did not give birth to three sons of different races, but rather, Noah gave birth to three sons who were the three ethnic originators from whom the nations of this world emanated.

Biblical/Historical Timeline

4000 BCE
God Creates Adam

2350 BCE
Noah Sons begin to Re-populate Earth

All dates and times are approximated based on accessible history, and biblical and secular records available.

I must call your attention to the date on the timeline that represents the approximate date that Noah's three sons begin to repopulate the earth. Three pertinent facts should be noted.

1. This is after the flood so only Noah's family is inhabitanting of the earth.
2. Noah and his family entered the ark at a location that was east of Eden on the continent of Africa
3. Noah lived a total of 950 years, but this timeline is attempting to position the start of his sons families, therefore the point on the timeline would be more indicative of the latter of Noah's days.

Just doing the math we see that from Adam's creation at approximately 4000 BCE until Noah's three sons begin to repopulate the earth at approximately 2350 BCE, there is a time length of 1,650 years. During this time, the entire world's population resided on the continent of Africa and the world's population was increasing until the great flood; they all were together and spoke the same language (*this will be shown later*). There were no nations, no races of people, no nationalities of people, ALL OF THE PEOPLE WERE AFRICAN, THEREFORE ALL OF THE PEOPLE WERE BLACK! So, up to this point, **THE ENTIRE WORLD WAS BLACK**! And I am going to show you the responsibility that God placed with Black People and how Black People are responsible for much of what we recognize as the creation of civilization, humanity, and existence as we know it today.1650 years is the minimum time period that the entire population was black and resided on the continent of Africa. As we continue to highlight Black History according to the Bible, the time length will extend up to the point that that God established the nations.

Since the objective of this book is to reveal black history according to the Bible, and Ham is the father of the indigenous black people, I will begin by looking at the offspring of Noah's son Ham. According to scripture, Ham had four sons[15]:

1. Cush (Ethiopia)
2. Mizraim (Egypt)
3. Put (Libya)
4. Canaan (Israel/Palestine)

Also note that Israel/Palestine are not descendents of Canaan, but when Noah cursed Canaan, Canaan's homeland inheritance was taken away and God stated that Canaan's homeland would be given to Abraham's descendents.[16]

We will now look at the sons of Ham, or Noah's grandsons via Ham. Once again, this is covered in detail in **Biblically Black and Blessed**, so I will just insert a diagram from the book that shows this lineage.

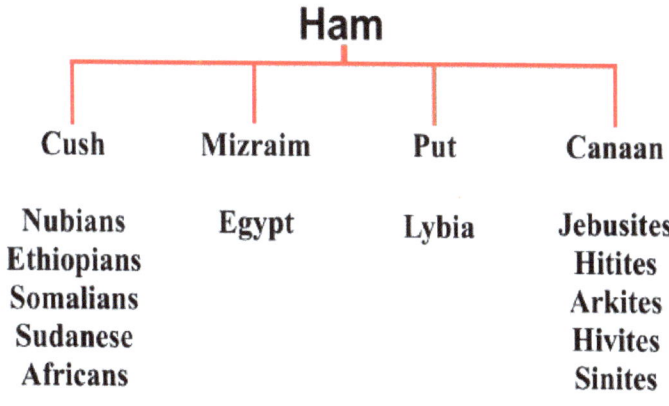

Ham

Cush	Mizraim	Put	Canaan
Nubians	Egypt	Lybia	Jebusites
Ethiopians			Hitites
Somalians			Arkites
Sudanese			Hivites
Africans			Sinites

---

[15] Genesis 10:6
[16] Genesis 17:8

SONS OF HAM AND THEIR
DIRECT DESCENDANTS

By looking at the graphic above, we see that the nations and people of Sub-Saharan Africa descended from Cush. In my **book Biblically Black and Bless II – The Children of The Ethiopians**, I show that in biblical times, all of the land below the Sahara Desert on the continent of Africa was known as Ethiopia. This designation for Sub-Saharan Africa continued until the seventeenth century[17].

Although some historians and Bible scholars point to documents that designate the entire continent of Africa as Ethiopia during biblical times, I do not adhere to this line of thinking because at times the Bible mentions Ethiopia, Egypt, and Libya (Put) as separate entities in the same text.[18]

> *"Ethiopia was her might, And Egypt too, without limits. Put and Lubim were among her helpers."*
> **Nahum 3:9**

But we will focus on Cush, because he is the father of the Sub-Saharan Africans. To do this, we will jump slightly ahead in the book of Genesis to Cush's son Nimrod.

> *8. And Cush begat Nimrod: he began to be a mighty one in the earth.*

---

[17] South African History Online –

[18] Ezekiel 30:5

9. He was a mighty hunter before the LORD: wherefore it is said, Even as Nimrod the mighty hunter before the LORD.
10. And the beginning of his kingdom was Babel, and Erech, and Accad, and Calneh, in the land of Shinar.
11. From that land he went forth into Assyria, and built Nineveh and Rehoboth-Ir and Calah,
12. and Resen between Nineveh and Calah; that is the great city.

Genesis 10:8-10

I cannot speak truthfully about biblical Black History without focusing on Nimrod. Although there have been numerous attempts to discredit Nimrod, the truth is that he was a God fearing historic figure in the progression of humanity throughout all of the earth. As the Bibles says, Nimrod was a mighty man throughout all of the earth. Nimrod was "a mighty hunter before the Lord". After the flood, God said to Noah that He had been given all of the animals for food.

3. Every moving thing that is alive shall be food for you; I give all to you, as I gave the green plant.
4. Only you shall not eat flesh with its life, that is, its blood.

Genesis 9:3-4

The time demanded strength, skill, and might to provide food and continue the progression of man. In Nimrod, God had His man. Nimrod was a "mighty hunter before the Lord". God recognized his hunting prowess, skill, and ability to provide food for the people. But even more than his ability as a hunter, Nimrod was a leader of the people as they continued their migration east from Eden. The scripture also says that Nimrod was a ruler with kingdoms that begin with Babel, Erech, Accad, and Calneh, in the Land of Shinar. He continued conquering and ruling nations, even Assyria, where he built Nineva, Rehoboth-Ir, and Calah. These, the Bible says were great cities. Many of the cities listed in scripture as cities founded or built by Nimrod were located in the Mesopotamia region of what we know today as the 'Middle East'. The earliest civilizations developed in this region between the Tigris and Euphrates River. This region was also known as 'Sumer' or the home of the Sumerians.

**MIDDLE EAST MAP WITH THE
MESOPOTAMIA CIRCLED IN RED**

In Sumerian history, Nimrod is known as King Etana of Kish. In the recorded 'King's List' that has been uncovered in archeological excavations in the Mesopotamia, King Etana (Nimrod) was the first King of Kish (Sumer) and he is described as "he who stabilized the lands." Sumerian history indicates that there is no other king that can compare to him in might. Another description of him in this king's list is that he was a man who "ascended to heaven." [19]Documented and recorded Sumerian history states that Nimrod was the first king and a powerful kingdom builder that wielded unmatched power and determination in his time. Being as great and mighty as he was, he became a legendary figure in Sumerian history. So the question has to be answered, if Nimrod was the African son of Cush, how did he arrive in the Mesopotamia region of the Middle East to begin his powerful reign as king of Kish? For the answer to this question, I will look to the eleventh chapter of Genesis. This chapter will not only provide the answer to this question, but it will provide clarity, enlightenment, and insight relative to the Black History.

If you recall, earlier I noted the eastward migration of man after Adam and Eve were evicted from Eden. We saw clearly that God evicted Adam and Eve on the east side of the Eden, and later we saw that Cain migrated even farther east when he was evicted from the presence of God. In His eviction of Adam and Eve, God positioned them in the direction that He wanted them to go. And this direction was leading to a place where He had a plan to reconcile man back to Him after the fall of Adam. And you will see that Black People, or Africans, are central to this plan. So in the words of U.S. Supreme Court Justice William O. Douglas, *"Go East Young Man, Go East."*

> *"1. Now the whole earth used the same language and the same words.*
> *2. It came about as they journeyed east, that they found a plain in the land of Shinar and settled there."*
> **Genesis 11:1-2**

---

[19] Dr. Samuel Noah Kramer - The Sumerians Their History, Culture, and Character p43

With the world's population experiencing unbridled growth, and the eastward migration of people since Adam and Eve were evicted from the east side of Eden, it wouldn't be long before this accelerated growth on land would reach the shores of the Red Sea. They already knew how to build vessels that could navigate the seas because Noah was required to build such a vessel during the flood. So the waters of the seas didn't inhibit the eastward migration of the people, their population continued to grow and they continued journeying east. The Bible states that they journeyed east and settled in a place known as the 'Land of Shinar." We know that the Land of Shinar was located in the southern Mesopotamia, or Sumer, and was the location of Sumerian cites that were built and founded by Nimrod; cities like Erech, Ur, and others. So the very first inhabitants of the southern Mesopotamia region of the world were Africans that journeyed east from the African continent into the lower, or southern, Mesopotamia. This fact is validated in Dr. Kramer's book on the Sumerians. In it he states that "it is reasonably certain that the first settlers in Sumer were not the Sumerians."[20]This would be true per the Bible as it states that the people of Africa journeyed east to the Land of Shinar, which is Sumer in the lower Mesopotamia. This became the birthplace of the Sumerians, who are the offspring of the Africans that first settled there. Being the offspring of Africans born outside of Africa, their birthplace became their indigenous homeland; hence they are referred to as Sumerians, instead of Africans; much like black people born in America today are Americans, not Africans. But since our ancestry and heritage is African, we retain our connection to the place of our ancestry by being called

---

[20] Dr. Samuel Noah Kramer – The Sumerians, Their History, Culture, and Character pp40

"African Americans". So likewise, these Sumerians should also be called "African Sumerians".

MAP OF AFRICA AND THE MIDDLE EAST REGION WITH SUMER OR THE LAND OF SHINAR REPRESENTED BY THE RED DOT

It is in this land that civilization as we know it today formed and accelerated.

The Sumerian people were indeed special people. God selected them to be the commencement of modern civilization and they begin as a people from Africa with Nimrod, the African son of Cush, as their leader. Keep in mind that at this point, there still are no races of people, no different ethnicities of people, and no nations. They are only people from Africa, and they are migrating east; God also

33

notes that they are one people[21] that spoke the same language. And it was in this environment that Nimrod and the Africans that journeyed east with him shined. They were brilliant people. They had to be brilliant because God had placed so much of the future of this world in their hands. The responsibilities that God assigned to these relocated Africans, or African Sumerians, (*even though they had relocated to the southern Mesopotamia, they were yet Africans*) was immense. But as I will show later, they lived up to God's assignment for them in a very BIG way!

THE SUMERIANS

According to World History Encyclopedia:

"the Sumerians were the people of southern Mesopotamia whose civilization flourished between 4100-1750 BCE. Their name comes from the region which is frequently – and incorrectly – referred to as a country".

The Bible states that Nimrod was the leader of these Sumerian people.[22]We all know Nimrod from his famed attempt to build a tower to heaven. He organized the people, (*who we now know to be the Sumerians*), and they proceeded to build a tower (*ziggurat*) that would reach heaven.[23]It is interesting how God dealt with their approach to build this tower. God said "the people are one and they all have the same language. "This speaks to what I stated above; the people of Sumer are Africans that journeyed into the lower Mesopotamia. They are not different nations. They are not different races. They are all one people. THEY ARE

---

21 Genesis 11:6
22 Genesis 10:10
23 Genesis 11:1-9

AFRICANS! They speak the African dialect. But God goes even further in describing these Africans. He specifically states of their attempt to build the tower to heaven, "And this is what they began to do, and now nothing which they purpose to do will be impossible for them."[24]Note here that God does not characterize the people as being evil, nor does He classify their attempt to build a tower to heaven as evil, God says that because they are determined to accomplish this feat, it would not be impossible for them. God says that anything that they purpose to do they will be able to do it. And since this is something that He did not want them to do, He confused their language so that they could not understand each other. And being confused by the various languages, they could not work together and finish the tower. It was at this time that God scattered them across the world. It was at this time that the nations of the world began to come into existence. So we can reasonably and confidently extend the time that the entire world was black even further to the failed attempt to build the tower of Babel.

For this I must make another entry onto the timeline with a time period note. If you note the entry, at about 2150 BCE Nimrod and the African people for which he was the leader attempted to build the Tower of Babel. This is when God scattered the people across the world, so my note on the timeline indicating when the world was black extends slightly beyond the time of the failed tower attempt because the people that were scattered were of direct African heritage, and it would be at least one generation in their new lands before they would be characterized as being indigenous to the new lands in which they settled. In their settling into their new lands, they would become nations themselves.

---

[24] Genesis 11:6

So the entire world was African from Adam to the failed attempt to build the tower of Babel. Or in other words, for approximately 2000 years, **THE WORLD WAS BLACK!**

Biblical/Historical Timeline

When The World Was Black

4000 BCE
God Creates Adam

2150 BCE
Noah's Great Grandson Nimrod attempts to build the Tower of Babel"

2350 BCE
Noah Sons begin to Re-populate Earth

All dates and times are approximated based on accessible history, and biblical and secular records available.

37

But for this section of this chapter, I want to focus on the Sumerians. These are the Africans that journeyed east from Africa and settled in the Land of Shinar. As stated earlier, these Africans were brilliant people. Even God acknowledged their brilliance when he said "***nothing which they purpose to do will be impossible for them***."History tells us that the accomplishments of these re-located African people during that time are inarguable proof that they considered no task to be impossible! We are very familiar with the attempt to build a tower to heaven. This attempt alone and God's reckoning that if these people were left alone, they would successfully complete the task, puts the engineering ability and skill of these people on display. But the brilliance of these African Sumerians is exhibited in the many creations, inventions, discoveries, and historical firsts that they are credited with. These history making creations, discoveries, and inventions set the boundaries of life as we know it today. These history making creations, discoveries, and inventions established the civilization that we currently live in. And they are all credited to the Sumerian people, the people who travelled east from Africa and settled in Sumer, the lower Mesopotamia, or as the Bible also calls it, The Land of Shinar. In another one of his books '***History Begins at Sumer***', Dr. Samuel Noah Kramer, one of the world's leading Assyriologists, and an expert in Sumerian history and Sumerian language, writes in detail about thirty-nine firsts that are attributed to the Sumerian people that established the civilization of the world. Although I have researched other Sumerian history documents, I have been referencing Dr. Kramer's research because of its completeness, its impeccable sources, and the firsthand documentation from his many archeological excavations in the region. So throughout this book, I will continue to reference Dr. Kramer for the majority of Sumerian source information that is external to the Bible. As I read his research, I was stunned at how closely the history that he documented from the era of early humans so closely matched the information in the Bible. But knowing that the Sumerians people were Africans who journeyed east filled my heart with pride. I beamed knowing that the people of my ancestral homeland were entrusted with such a tremendous responsibility as establishing civilization.

The thirty-nine firsts of man's recorded history that came be attributed to the Africans who travelled east and settled in the Lower Mesopotamia, or the Sumerians are indications of the brilliance of the people that Nimrod lead. These creations, discoveries, and inventions established life as we know it today. I will not list all of the thirty-nine firsts documented by Dr. Kramer, but I will list a few of the most impactful firsts to civilization; civilization creating firsts that make it possible for us to enjoy a functional, pleasant, and progressive existence today.

The First Schools Libraries – The scientific, historical, and archeological finds all indicate that it was the African people who travelled east and settled in the southern Mesopotamia that are responsible for establishing the first educational system implemented to teach. This was a direct outgrowth of their invention of Cuneiform writing.

The Invention of Writing – At the heart of the many creations and inventions that these relocated Africans are responsible for is Cuneiform writing, or simply, writing. The ability to document and preserve oral communications could be the most impactful contribution to modern society that has ever been made.

The First Government – Nimrod was the first ruler (king) of the Sumerian land and documents uncovered from the many scientific excavations into the lower Mesopotamia also show that the first establishment of government and political congress was convened there by the Sumerians.

This congress consisted on two houses, much like the congress of the United States has today.

The First Case of Tax Reduction – Sumerian documents indicate that tax reform was instituted as a form of Social Reform to correct the injustices by a prior ruling party that heavily and unjustly taxed the citizens of Sumer.

The First Legal System – With population growth and the progress of people, guidelines were needed to establish and define the personal parameters needed for the peaceful existence of all citizens.

The First Pharmacy – When a Sumerian physician decided to collect and record his most valuable medical prescriptions for his students, man's first pharmacy was established. His prescriptions were uncovered while on an archeological excavation in the southern Mesopotamia.

The First Farmer's Almanac – This is interesting, but documentation excavated from that era in time reveals instructions from a farmer that guided others through their annual agricultural activities utilizing knowledge of seasonal changes relative to the signs of the sky.

The First 24-Hour Clock – The Sumerians were responsible for establishing the time clock as we know it today. They segmented the day into 12 hours AM and 12 hours PM, created the 60-minute hour, and the 60 second minute.

The Use of a Signature for Personal Identification – This is also another off shoot of their invention of writing. The personal signature was established to uniquely associate individuals with activities, documents, and purposeful events. It was referred to as a *"cylinder seal"*. These seals were used by everyone, from royals to slaves, as a means of authenticating identity in correspondence

The First Ziggurat – The ziggurat, a rectangular stepped tower, is an impressive engineering marvel, even today. We became familiar with the ziggurat when we read of Nimrod's attempt to build one that would reach heaven.

Neither time nor space allows me to cover the complete list of creations, inventions, discoveries, etc. that are attributed to the Sumerians. There are numerous resources available that document much of this with credible sources. As stated earlier, I am primarily referencing the work of Dr. Samuel Kramer[25], but some of my sources can be attributed to the World History[26] site that provides details about the Sumerians.

As you can see from the brief list that I've included thus far, the contributions of these relocated Africans are the heart of our existence today. These contributions make living a comfortable, peaceable, and progressive life possible. And when any discussion of Black History occurs, or when Black History is taught, these contributions must be included and heralded as contributions made to society by Africans, people of African ancestry, or the Sumerians.

With so many important and life defining contributions to society made by the Sumerians, knowledge of them as a people should be prominent in black educational institutions, black religious institutions, and in black society as a whole. Sumerian history should be embraced as Black History. But why hasn't this happened, at least in black religious

---

[25] Dr. Samuel Noah Kramer -- History Begins at Sumer
[26] https://www.worldhistory.org/Sumerians/

institutions? This brings me to my next sub-chapter within this chapter, The Misleadings of King James.

THE MISLEADINGS OF KING JAMES

A recent survey by Google trends revealed what many Believers have always known to be true. The King James Bible continues to be the most popular and utilized English translations of scripture[27] in the world. This is the Bible that was used to teach and train most African Americans. It is also the Bible that our ancestors were programmed with almost immediately after being taken from slave ships, sold as property, and being locating on plantations. It is the Bible that King Leopold used to justify the slaughter of more than ten million Africans in the Congo. It is the Bible used by Hitler to justify his brutal, vicious, and deadly attack on the Jews. It is the Bible used by the KKK to justify their superiority as a race. Need I say more? The King James Bible purports itself as scripture, but is it really? Better yet, is any Bible version actually scripture? The Apostle Paul writes to Timothy saying:

> *"All Scripture is inspired by God and profitable for teaching, for reproof, for correction, for training in righteousness;"*
> **2 Timothy 3:16**

According to Paul, scripture is the text that is inspired by God. Those texts are documented and preserved in the native languages of the individuals that were divinely inspired to write them. Therefore, scripture is the Hebrew, Greek, and Aramaic texts that were inspired by God. The books that we,

---

[27]https://10bibleverses.com/scripture-quotes/most-popular-english-bible-translations-2022-scripture-statistics/

those of us who do not read, write, or speak the native languages, know as Bibles are really translations. They are what the translators have told us that the scripture says. Being as such, the influences, biases, prejudices, and educational inadequacies of the translators can have an enormous impact on the veracity of what we actually receive as inspired text. We could actually be receiving text that is characterized as 'inspired' when in fact it is only the opinion of the translator. Therefore, it is important that we, as people who do not communicate in the native languages of scripture, understand that what we are reading is a translation of the inspired text, and not the inspired text. With that being said, I will reveal the Misleading of the King James translators as it relates to the original people travelling out of Africa; the very people that God entrusted with starting civilization and establishing society. And with this I will show how a single mislead in the King James translation, (the insertion of two words into the inspired text), can dismiss an entire people, characterize them as irrelevant in God's plan, and thereby minimize, to the world, the prominence of their relationship with their creator. I will start by looking at Genesis chapter eleven, verse two.

> *"It came about as they journeyed east, that they found a plain in the land of Shinar and settled there."*
>
> **Genesis 11:2 NASB**

As you can see, the NASB states that the people journeyed east into the land of Shinar. I use the NASB because it is recognized as the most accurate word for word translation of scripture from the languages of the original text. In the following graphic, you see the map from earlier highlighting the location of the Land of Shinar in the southern Mesopotamia. You can also see that if people are journeying east into the Land of Shinar, they would be coming from the west. And west of the southern Mesopotamia is the continent of Africa. So according to the God inspired text, the people were coming from the west and headed east. If you recall from earlier in this book, this movement would also be consistent with the eastward movement of the people after Adam and Eve were evicted from Eden on the east side. We then saw Cain move ever further eastward. Therefore Genesis 11:2 is a continuation of the eastward movement that begin when God evicted Adam and Eve from Eden. But this is not how the King James translators translated this verse. They added two words to the inspired text that completely changed the direction that the people travelled. This is how King James translated this verse.

> *"And it came to pass, as they journeyed from the east, that they found a plain in the land of Shinar; and they dwelt there."*
>
> **Genesis 11:2 KJV**

Note how they have added the words "from the" to the inspired text, and therewith changed the direction of travel to be opposite of what God said. So according to King James, the people are travelling from the east, or moving west into the Land of Shinar. A quick look at a map reveals that east of the Land of Shinar is Eurasia, or Asia and Europe. With the addition of those two words, King James has the original people coming from Europe or Asia instead of Africa.

TRAVELLING EAST INTO SHINAR (BLACK ARROW) VS. TRAVELLING FROM THE EAST INTO SHINAR (RED ARROW)

So all of the contributions to humanity and the developments and inventions that established civilization either came from people who came into the southern Mesopotamia from Africa or they came from people who migrated into the southern Mesopotamia from Eurasia.

Let's take a closer look at this verse.

Here is the Hebrew text for Genesis 11:2

וַיְהִי, בְּנָסְעָם מִקֶּדֶם; וַיִּמְצְאוּ בִקְעָה בְּאֶרֶץ שִׁנְעָר, וַיֵּשְׁבוּ שָׁם.

I have underlined the Hebrew phrase in the verse that speaks to the direction that the people travelled. This phrase has been examined and analyzed by numerous Hebrew scholars, and they all say that this phrase represents the English words "journeyed east". So how the King James translators arrived at "journeyed from the east" is suspicious at best. Most of the other translations that are taken directly from the Hebrew also translate this as "journeyed east". Here is the verse as translated by a few of the most used translations.

As the people migrated to the east, they found a plain in the land of Babylonia and settled there. (NLT)

As people moved eastward, they found a plain in Shinar and settled there. (NIV)

And it came about, as they journeyed east, that they found a plain in the land of Shinar and settled there. (NASB)

And as people journeyed eastward, they found a plain in the land of Shinar and they settled there. (Amplified)

And it came to pass, as they journeyed east, that they found a plain in the land of Shinar; and they dwelt there. (ASV)

At first I dismissed this as an unintentional error by the King
James translators, but after further examination, I find it hard
to believe that the error was unintentional. For in Genesis
13:11, the same Hebrew phrase appears and there the King
James translators made the correct translation.

Here is Genesis 13:11 in the King James Version

> "*Then Lot chose him all the plain of Jordan; and
> Lot journeyed east:*"
>
> **Genesis 13:11 KJV**

Here is the Hebrew text for Genesis 13:11

וַיִּבְחַר־לֹו לֹוט אֵת כָּל־כִּכַּר הַיַּרְדֵּן וַיִּסַּע לֹוט מִקֶּדֶם וַיִּפָּרְדוּ
אִישׁ מֵעַל אָחִיו:

Once again, I underlined the portion of the verse that
identifies the direction of travel. And you can see that it is
the exact same Hebrew phase that appears in Genesis 11:2.
It then becomes obvious that the King James translators
knew what the phrase meant, because they made a correct
translation here. And as you can see, the Hebrew phrase is
exactly the same for both verses, but King James translates
them as opposite direction.

So King James translates the exact same Hebrew phrase as opposite directions.

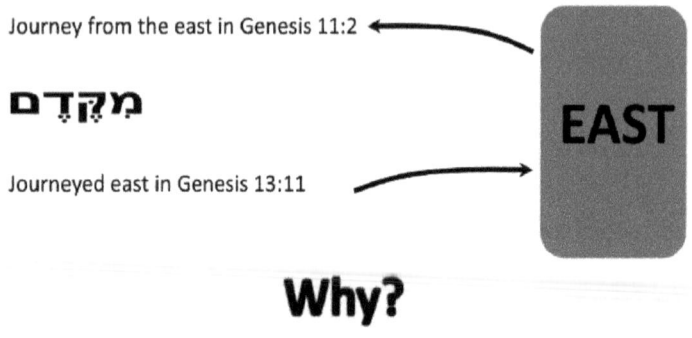

Journey from the east in Genesis 11:2

מִקֶּ֫דֶם

Journeyed east in Genesis 13:11

EAST

Why?

I will leave it up to the reader to draw any conclusions as to why the King James translators modified God's divinely inspired text, but the impact that the modification has had on how African people and people of African ancestry have been viewed throughout the ages has been enormous. By changing the direction that the people travelled, King James effectively diminished the importance of Africans and people of African ancestry to humanity. The credit for all of the creations, developments, and inventions that emanated from the Africans that journeyed east were taken away and given to people from Eurasia. This misleading modification dismissed the role that Africans and people of African ancestry had in establishing modern civilization. The addition of two words into the divinely inspired text mischaracterized a nation of brilliant people as ignorant and uncivilized. But most importantly, the misinterpretation of this verse eliminated the role that God assigned to the descendants of Noah's son Ham. But the world would not be what it is today had not God sent those Africans east to start civilization.

There may be numerous explanations for why the King James translators changed the direction of travel of God's original people into The Land of Shinar, but what cannot be disputed is that they manipulated the divinely inspired text, and in doing this they then translated the exact same Hebrew phrase as two different directions. This manipulation of the divinely inspired text diminished God's purpose, plan, and relationship with the people on the continent of Africa and their descendants. I have been a user of the King James Bible for almost all of my life as a Believer, well over 45 years. And there have been other issues with KJV that I've had to explain, but the criticality of the error of Genesis 11:2 caused me to move away from that version. Today I use a more accurate translation for my sermons, lessons, classes, conferences, etc.

I will close this chapter with a quote from Dr. Jonathan R. Zinskind, Associate Professor of Ancient History at Notre Dame University.

"The mystery surrounding the people who formed the Harrapa and Mohenjo-Daro (Sumerian) culture in the Indus valley would be cleared up if the language and the culture could be deciphered. With respect to Sumer, it was the decipherment that created the problem."

In Dr. Zinskind's statement, he indicates that the problem with understanding Sumerian culture is the decipherment of their language. But it was this very language that God confounded.[28]

the BLACK NATIONS

So the LORD scattered them abroad from thence upon the face of
all the earth: and they left off to build the   city.

Genesis 11:8

We have arrived at the point where God purposes to locate
the nations in the lands for which they have kingdom and
purpose assignments. God purposes to disperse the people to
distant lands across the globe from the Land of Shinar, which
is also known as the lower or southern Mesopotamia; and in
world history, it is known as Sumer, or the home to the
Sumerians. But keep in mind that the people of this land are
the Africans that "journeyed east" as a result of God
positioning them for eastward migration when He evicted
Adam and Eve from Eden.

Nimrod, the son of Cush, who is the leader of these Africans
that journeyed out of Africa into the southern Mesopotamia,
determines to build a tower to heaven. Although much has

been written of this plan to elevate humanity to the place where God resides, most of what has been written is simply conjecture. And if we are truthful, this conjecture was created to demonize Nimrod, dismiss the strong relationship that Africans enjoyed with their creator, and mischaracterize Africans as uncivilized, evil, and inhumane. The strong relationship that Africans and those of African ancestry enjoy with the creator has been a life sustaining relationship that has preserved us as a people in the face of so much hatred and opposition. Nowhere in the divinely inspired scripture is anything evil mentioned about Nimrod. The fact is that all of the scriptures mentioning Nimrod state that he was mighty before the Lord, and a kingdom builder that built historic cities. Scripture presents Nimrod as leader that ensured the survival of his constituents. Nimrod was just the type of leader that God needed as He prepared His people to migrate to their indigenous homelands. I'm sure that Abraham carried much knowledge acquired from Nimrod when he, accompanying his father, left the lower Mesopotamia and headed west towards Canaan. There will be much more on Abraham's migration later.

When God did not want Nimrod to build the tower of Babel, God confused their language and scattered the people forth from 'The Land of Shinar' to settle in distant places in the world.

> " 8. So the LORD scattered them abroad from thence upon the face of all the earth: and they left off to build the city.
> 9. Therefore is the name of it called Babel; because the LORD did there confound the language of all the earth: and from thence did the LORD scatter them abroad upon the face of all the earth."
>
> **Genesis 11:8-9**

At this time, nation building begins. Until now the people had been one people (African), they all spoke the same language, and they were unified in thought and purpose (they were one). This has been shown in the previous pages of this book by referencing the verses of Genesis chapter eleven. I cannot overemphasize that these people were the African people that continued the eastward migratory path that God started them on. Looking back to this time in the history of man, the Apostle Paul explained it like this.

> " *He made from one man every nation of mankind to live on all the face of the earth, having determined their appointed times and the boundaries of their habitation,*"
>
> **Acts 17:26**

Considering the location where Adam was created, then the location where, some two thousand years later, the people were sent out to establish the nations of the world, I can't help but to conclude that the wisdom of God is wiser than the wisdom of man, and God's impeccable plan to establish His kingdom on earth is indeed infallible. In my book '**Biblically Black and Blessed – God's Relationship With Black People'**, I provide the output of exhaustive research into the Biblical origin of the nations of the world as we know them today. In my second book on this subject '**Biblically Black and Blessed II– The Children of The Ethiopians***, "* I explain to which nation that the people who settled on the African continent below the Sahara Desert are of. For this book, I will not repeat this detail. Biblically Black and Blessed 1 and 2 are recommended resources for this information.

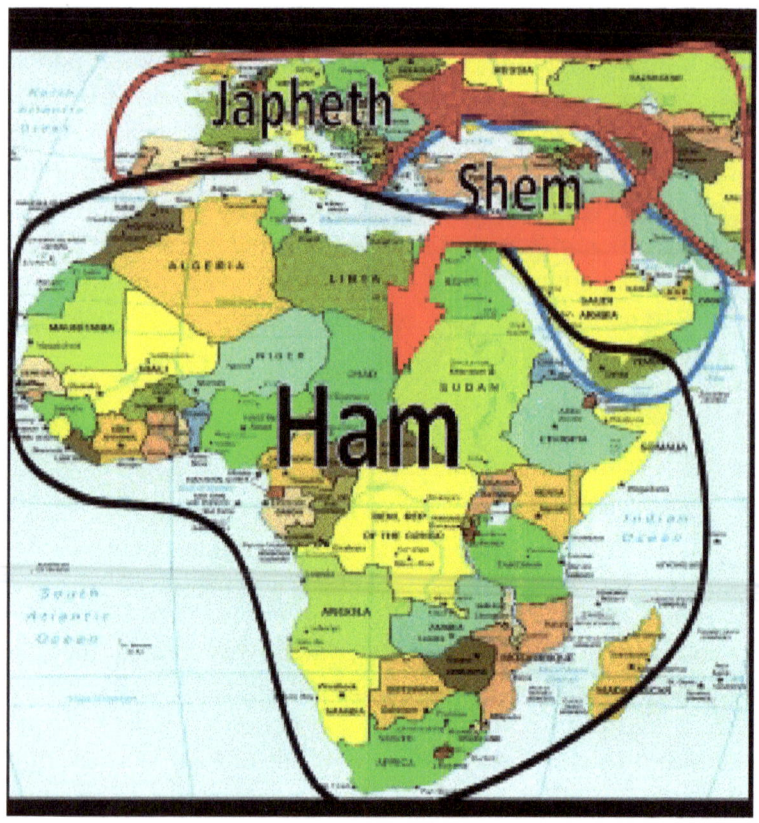

**MAP SHOWING THE MIGRATION OUT
OF THE LAND OF SHINAR**

I use The Land of Shinar, or the Lower Mesopotamia, as the starting point for the dispersion of the nations because of Genesis Chapter 11. However, as the people Journeyed eastward from the point of creation, not all of the people had to go into the Land of Shinar, some could have settled in the lands of Africa as others migrated. But it is at the Land of Shinar, or the Lower Mesopotamia, where many descendants of all three of Noah's sons migrated east to; this is also where, as I covered earlier, Nimrod established the first human kingdom with government oversight. And as we saw earlier, this is also where so many contributions to life as we know it today were created, discovered, invented, and first implemented. Many of the utilities that we are accustomed to today were created/invented/established in this "Land of Shinar" during this time. This knowledge must be included in any discussion, lesson, message, book, etc. relative to Black History and credit must be properly given to the people of Africa for these life-defining contributions to the world. The map above depicts the early migration of man at a very high level; I will re-visit it later because it provides insight into God's plan for the establishment of His Kingdom on earth. I will also zoom in closer as we see the family of Abraham being sent away from the Land of Shinar.

As the people were dispersed, there is evidence that the Shemites and the Hamites continued to recognize the Supreme Being and give credit to this higher power as the responsible entity for the world and creation. But the Japhethites, seeking to elevate themselves above the other nations, rejected this idea, declaring themselves to be superior[29] and changed the image of the Supreme Being to their benefit[30]. To understand this, we must acknowledge the calling of the Apostle Paul (Apostle to the Gentiles[31]), and comprehensively analyze his writings. Paul was the Apostle chosen by God to minister the gospel to the Gentiles. Throughout his ministration to the Gentiles, The Apostle Paul reveals the character of Japheth's descendants (the Gentiles)[32] and why there was a need to send an apostle to reconnect them to their creator. They had deviated from the inherent reverence of God and were even worshipping

---

[29] Matthew 20:25-26
[30] Romans 1:21-23
[31] Romans 11:13, Ephesians 3:1, Galatians 1:15-16
[32] Genesis 10:2-5

Satan.[33] But I must return to the creation of the nations. The history of the Gentiles is a topic for another time and book. As the people are exiting the Land of Shinar and travelling to the places where they will establish nations, God directs Abraham's father to take his family and head west. This was not a hap-hazard, uncontrolled scattering that occurs when danger forces a crowd to disperse, seeking safety. But rather, God directed the people and groups to areas in the world to fulfill their purpose and carry out their assignment in His kingdom on earth. Just as God said to Abram, *"Get thee out of thy country, and from thy kindred, and from thy father's house, unto a land that I will shew thee:"*[34], this would also be the way in which He directed every people/group away from The Land of Shinar to the area in which they would settle and become indigenous.

Looking at our Biblical Timeline, we see that God called Abram from his father's house in Haran shortly after the failed attempt to build the tower of Babel and at the time that the nations started dispersing from the land of Shinar.

> *"31. Now Terah took his son Abram, and Lot the son of Haran, his grandson, and his daughter-in-law Sarai, his son Abram's wife, and they departed together from Ur of the Chaldeans to go to the land of Canaan; and they went as far as Haran and settled there.*
> *32. The days of Terah were 205 years; and Terah died in Haran."*
>
> **Genesis 11:31-32**

---

[33] 1 Corinthians 10:20
[34] Genesis 12:1

The city of Ur of the Chaldeans was a city in the Land of Shinar, also known as Sumer in the lower or southern Mesopotamia. I must strongly emphasize a prominent message of this book that is verified with scripture and documented with world history. The people who are being sent out from the Land of Shinar to start the nations of the world are the Africans that journeyed east in Genesis 11:2. Since they no longer reside on the continent of Africa, the Land of Shinar became known as Sumer and the people were reclassified as Sumerians. Hence, the Sumerians were Africans that migrated off the continent towards the east. It may be beneficial to start referring to these people as African Sumerians, much like people of African ancestry in the United States today are referred to as African Americans. I started designating these people as African Sumerians earlier in this book, and this will be my designation for them going forward.

With this, we must make another entry and note to our timeline.

NOTE:
It is important to note here that Moses is recording this history of Genesis in what is clearly centuries after it actually happened. At the time of the scatter, NO ONE KNEW THE REQUIREMENTS OF GOD BECAUSE GOD HAD NOT PROVIDED THEM AT THE TIME! The ability to hear and be led of God is a result of man possessing a **soul**. It is the **soul** that connects us to God and makes every man a child of God. So even without knowledge of God, man can become sensitive to and hear the voice of God and receive unctions or leadings via our soul connection to the creator.[35] This is explained with comprehension in the book "*Winning Spiritual Wars*".

_____

[35] Romans 1:20-32

So in The Land of Shinar, when God scattered the people/groups, they could have received an unction from the LORD, or maybe the LORD, who is a spirit, appeared and spoke to their souls, which is them in the spiritual world. They may have been given dreams; but regardless of the way that God communicated with them, we see that God had an obvious plan for bringing people to their indigenous residential destinations.

Biblical/Historical Timeline

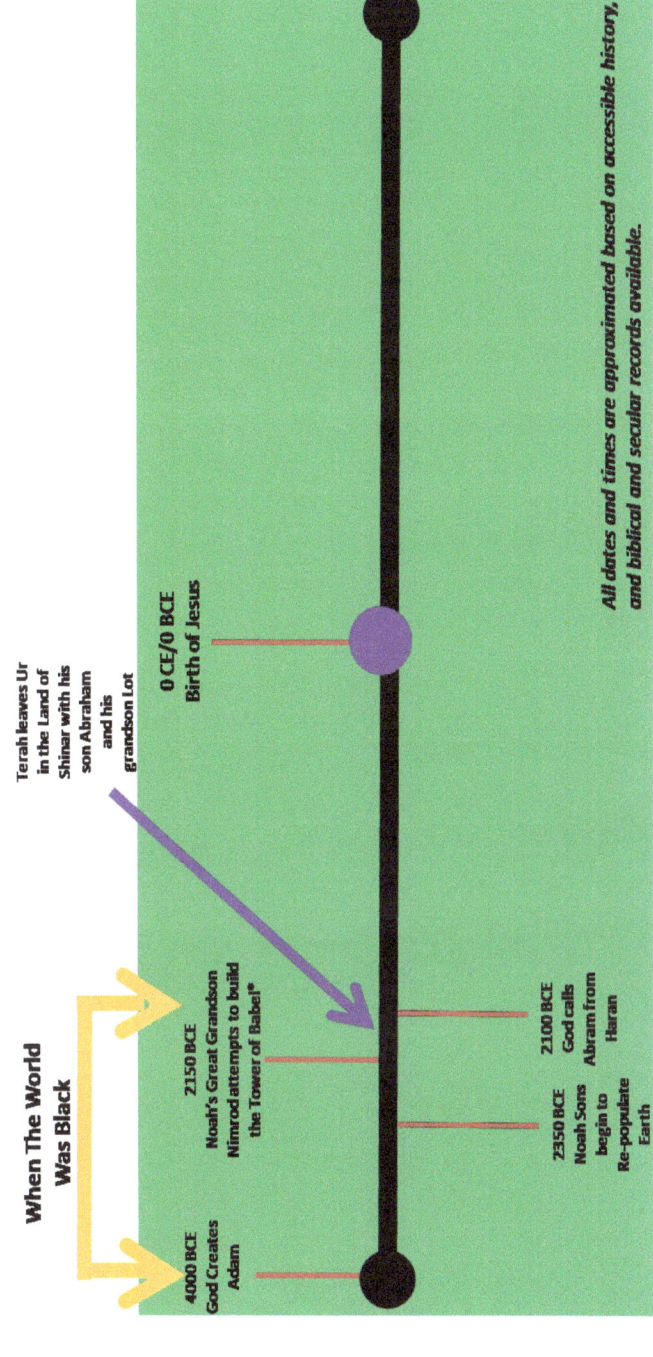

When The World Was Black

4000 BCE
God Creates Adam

2350 BCE
Noah Sons begin to Re-populate Earth

2150 BCE
Noah's Great Grandson Nimrod attempts to build the Tower of Babel*

2100 BCE
God calls Abram from Haran

Terah leaves Ur in the Land of Shinar with his son Abraham and his grandson Lot

0 CE/0 BCE
Birth of Jesus

All dates and times are approximated based on accessible history, and biblical and secular records available.

With this note we can perform a few rough math calculations and derive a few pertinent facts. Since we know that the life expectancy was shortened to one hundred and twenty years shortly before the great flood.[36] And we previously created an entry on the timeline that represents the approximate time that Noah's three sons begin re-populating the earth. Earlier in this book, we used the genealogical tables in Genesis chapters 5 and 10 to approximate the time of Abraham's birth. With this information we can conclude that Abraham's grandfather, possibly his great grandfather, journeyed east with the group mentioned in Genesis 11:2. It was most likely Abraham's grandfather when considering the normal lifespan of 120 years. This was also confirmed with the following statement found in Dr. Kramer's book 'The Sumerians, Their History, Culture, and Character[37]:

> *"there may very well have been considerable Sumerian blood in Abraham's forefathers, who lived for generation in Ur or some other Sumerian cities"*
>
> **Dr. Samuel Noah Kramer**

We know that Abraham was an African Sumerian because he lived with his father in the city of Ur, and Ur is a historically documented Sumerian city. This ties the genealogy of Abraham back to Africa through 'The Land of Shinar". But Abraham ancestry not only connects him to Africa, but to Sub-Saharan Africa, the place where Eden was located, and the place where Adam and Eve began this journey of humanity. The people of Sub-Saharan Africa have darker skin than they of northern Africa. In my book

---

[36] Genesis 6:3
[37] The Sumerians, Their History, Culture, and Character pp299

Biblically Black and Blessed – What The Bible Says About God's Relationship With Black People, I reference the work of Dr. Nina Jablonski, an American anthropologists whose scientific work explains the variations in human skin color and pigmentation as inherent human adaptive characteristics, making the people suitable for survival in the environment in which they settled. In other words, over time, people skin color and pigmentation adapted for survival in the environment in which they lived. This would account for Japheth's descendants having lighter skin and hairier bodies as they settled in cold places far away from the sun's ultraviolent rays. Likewise, this would explain the descendants of Ham becoming darker and less hairy as they settled into the lands closest to the sun's ultraviolent rays, as well as Shem's descendants having skin color that has color somewhere between the skin color of Ham's descendants and Japheth's descendants. And since Shem descendants indigenous homeland is in close proximity with Mizraim's and Phut's homeland, they would look like brothers even though they descended from different sons of Noah. God uses this likeness to safely protect the baby Jesus when King Herod sought His life.

I must re-emphasize that at the time that the people journeyed into the Land of Shinar, God had not given His instructions and requirements to them, so they only knew of a Supreme Being to whom they credited all of the things that they acknowledged, experienced, and witnessed that they knew they couldn't/didn't control. So in an attempt to credit this Supreme Being, they created statues of wood, stubble, gold, etc. to represent the God of whom they had no knowledge. This is the time period to which the Apostle Paul alluded to while in Athens in the 17th chapter of Acts

"29. Therefore, since we are the descendants of God, we ought not to think that the Divine Nature is like gold or silver or stone, an image formed by human skill and thought.
30. So having overlooked the times of ignorance, God is now proclaiming to mankind that all people everywhere are to repent"

Acts 17:29-30

In all of the research that I have conducted on the Sumerians, one thing stands out and stands tall. **The numerous figures, statues, monuments, etc. that they used to represent God.**

However, these monuments, statues, figures, etc., were **NOT** attempts to replace the LORD (*of whom they had no knowledge*), but rather these were the results of highly intelligent people that were becoming even more knowledgeable and therefore seeking answers to questions about things that they understood were well beyond their control. They knew that there had to be a power greater than they, they just had no direct knowledge of this power. They knew of a Supreme Being that was greater than they because as Paul wrote:

"19. because that which is known about God is evident within them; for God made it evident to them.
20. For since the creation of the world His invisible attributes, that is, His eternal power and divine nature, have been clearly perceived, being understood by what has been made, so that they are without excuse."

Romans 1:19-20

62

God, realizing their ignorance, winked at it as He sent Abraham west to Canaan and commenced His plan to provide instructions and knowledge of Him to the entire world through the lineage of Abraham.

During the time of dispersing the people to their indigenous homelands to establish the nations, God winked at their ignorance when they created so many images to represent Him, but He also had a plan to reveal Himself to them and provide His instructions and guidance to them; and Abraham and His descendents would be the center point of this plan for mankind receiving correct knowledge of God. So as God was scattering the nations, He appears to Abraham in Haran, (*a land north of Canaan*) and sent him south to Canaan.[38]

Let's take what we now know and drive home a very pertinent point.

What the Bible tells us about Abraham prior to being called by God along with what documented scientific research validates lets us know that before there were nations or ethnic nationalities, Abraham lived as an African Sumerian in Ur, a city in the Land of Shinar. This means that Abraham departed from the Land of Shinar with Terah (his father) when all the people were one (*Genesis 11:1,6*), thereby making Abraham a resident of the earth during the time when the whole world was of African ethnic identity. In other words...

ABRAHAM WAS BLACK!

Abraham was an African Sumerian, and he was so proud of his heritage that connected him with the people of Africa, that when he was old and nearing death, he made his servant take an oath that he would return to the southern

---

[38] Genesis 12:1-3

Mesopotamia, or the land of the African Sumerians, to select a wife for his son Isaac.[39]

And from this point, the focus of the Bible is almost exclusively focused on the descendants of Abraham because of their assignment in God's plan. They were to receive the instructions (oracles as Paul referred this[40]) from God and teach this to the nations of the world.

However, we get great insight into the descendants of Ham by examining the numerous times that they interacted with Israel, and we get an even clearer picture of the descendants of Japheth, (the Gentiles) from the Apostle Paul. So the additions to our timeline from this point until the birth of Jesus will consist of Ham's descendants **MAJOR** interactions with Abraham's descendants. Each of these interactions represents a Black History event in the annuls of biblical and world history. And for the believer of African ancestry, this Black History should be highlighted and passed down to successive generations with pride.

I will continue the timeline by adding an entry to each of the major times that Abraham or his descendents interacted with the descendants of Ham, because all of these interactions would be a Black History moments in the history of man.

But prior to continuing the timeline, let me introduce to you the Lemba people of Africa, because they too, are relevant to Black History According to God's Word.

THE LEMBA PEOPLE OF AFRICA

---

[39] Genesis chapter 24
[40] Romans 3:2

The Lemba People of Africa are Jewish people who yet reside on the continent of Africa. The Lemba, a tribe of 70,000 to 80,000 members who live in central Zimbabwe and northern South Africa, have customs which are similar to Jewish ones: Lemba refrain from eating pork or other foods forbidden by the Torah, or forbidden combinations of permitted foods, they wear yarmulke-like skull caps, conduct ritual animal slaughter, have a holy day once a week, and even put a Star of David on their gravestones.

Mitochondrial DNA testing validates their ethnic Jewish heritage, and their lifestyle verifies their dedication to God. As quoted from a New York Times article, "A team of geneticists has found that many Lemba men carry in their male chromosome a set of DNA sequences that is distinctive of the Cohanim, the Jewish priests believed to be the descendants of Aaron. The genetic signature of priests -- a hereditary caste, different from rabbis but with certain ritual roles -- is particularly common among Lemba men who belong to the senior of their 12 groups, known as the Buba clan."[41] This genetic testing was carried out by British scientists and it revealed that many of the Lemba tribesmen in southern Africa have Jewish origins.[42] According to Lemba oral history, a people known as the 'Buba clan' brought them out of Judah and from Israel to Africa.[43] This would place them in the direct lineage of Abraham and of

---

[41] New York Times --
https://www.nytimes.com/1999/05/09/us/dna-backs-a-tribe-s-tradition-of-early-descent-from-the-jews.html

[42] World Jewish Congress -
https://www.worldjewishcongress.org/en/news/lemba-tribe-in-southern-africa-has-jewish-roots-genetic-tests-reveal

[43] Lemba People,Wikipedia --
https://en.wikipedia.org/wiki/Lemba_people#:~:text=As%20re counted%20in%20Lemba%20oral,in%20the%20general%20J ewish%20population.

the tribe of Judah. So if you are searching for the biblical tribe of Judah today, look no further than the Lemba tribe of Sub-Saharan Africa!

ADDITIONAL BLACK HISTORY MOMENTS *of the* BIBLE

THE EGYPTIANS SAVE ABRAHAM

The very next entry into our timeline occurs at approximately 2075 BCE.

This Black History encounter is recorded in the twelfth chapter of Genesis.

It is shortly after God sends Abraham down to Canaan to establish what will become the Jewish state of Israel there. Shortly after Abraham arrived in Canaan, there was a severe famine in the land. An interesting observation of this encounter is that Abraham, as we know from the previous pages of this book, is an African Sumerian that has been sent by God to establish the Jewish nation in Canaan land. When the famine hits the land, he has to travel to Egypt and live there because they had food in great supply. If you recall from earlier in this book, Egypt is the indigenous African homeland of Ham's son Mizraim.

So in this interaction you see the African Mizraim (Egypt) preserving the life of the African Sumerian Abraham.

Of special note is how ethical and moral the Egyptian Pharaoh was in his dealings with Abraham and Sarah.

This indeed is a Black History Moment!

Biblical/Historical Timeline

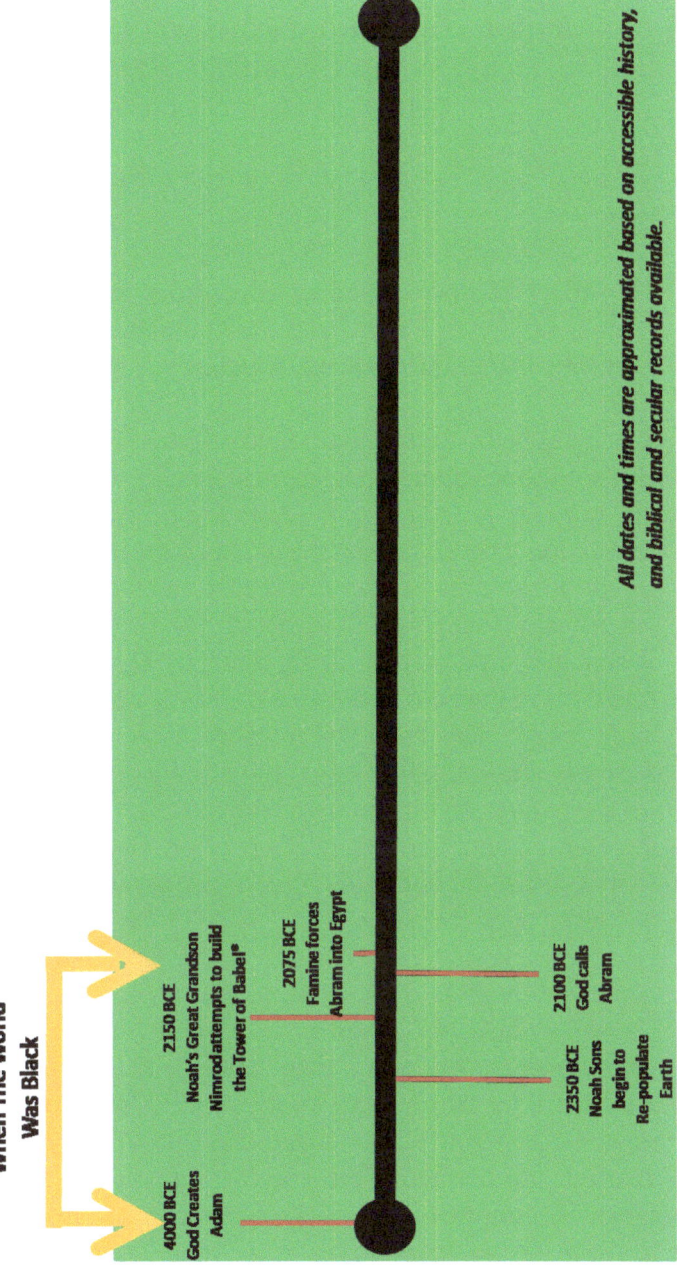

When The World Was Black

4000 BCE
God Creates Adam

2350 BCE
Noah Sons begin to Re-populate Earth

2150 BCE
Noah's Great Grandson Nimrod attempts to build the Tower of Babel*

2100 BCE
God calls Abram

2075 BCE
Famine forces Abram into Egypt

All dates and times are approximated based on accessible history, and biblical and secular records available.

THE EGYPTIANS SAVE JACOB AND BECOMES
THE LAND WHERE GOD WILL GROW
AND DEVELOP ISRAEL FROM A
FAMILY INTO A NATION.

This entry into our timeline occurs at approximately 1850 BCE.

This Black History encounter is recorded in the forty-sixth chapter of Genesis. However, the complete account of this starts at Chapter thirty-seven of Genesis.

Much has been written about the bondage of Israel in Egypt. But not enough attention is given to the fact that this bondage did not last as long as we believe, and this bondage was really God's hand, forcing the descendants of Jacob to leave Egypt. Jacob and his extended family entered Egypt because once again, there was a sever famine in their homeland. When they first arrived in Egypt, they enjoyed enormous freedoms in the land because of the favor that was bestowed upon Joseph. This favor and freedom allowed them to grow, develop, and multiply within Egypt. When it became time for them to return to their own homeland and begin fulfilling their assignment within God's kingdom, God let a king rise to power that did not know Joseph; hence the favor that was bestowed upon them because of Joseph was taken away. And because they were growing and developing, this new king perceived them as a threat to his power, so he made them slaves within his country. So with being in Egypt approximately 400 years, their bondage really didn't begin until the king that had no knowledge of Joseph came into power. So their actual bondage was approximately 80-100 years. But in rehearsing the story of Israel in Egypt, so many times we omit this grace and hospitality that Egypt showed to them for hundreds of years; we tend to forget how they were allowed to grow and develop in Egypt. We tend to overlook the sustenance that was provided when famine forced Jacob there. We forget the grace that was shown to Moses as he was being prepared to lead his people out of Egypt. We even dismiss the fact that it was God that installed the king that did not know Joseph so that Israel would be forced to leave and start their kingdom work.

God had to force Israel out of Egypt in this way because they were comfortable in Egypt. They had what they wanted, their needs were being supplied, they lived a peaceable existence there; as long as they were doing well, there was no need to leave. They were living large in Egypt. So God inserted a king of Egypt that dealt harshly with them in their latter years in the country. This harsh treatment forced them to seek relief, and their relief was to be found in their own country.

The entry on the timeline represents the approximate time of Jacobs entry into Egypt. The beginning of the approximate 400 years that they were there.

Biblical/Historical Timeline

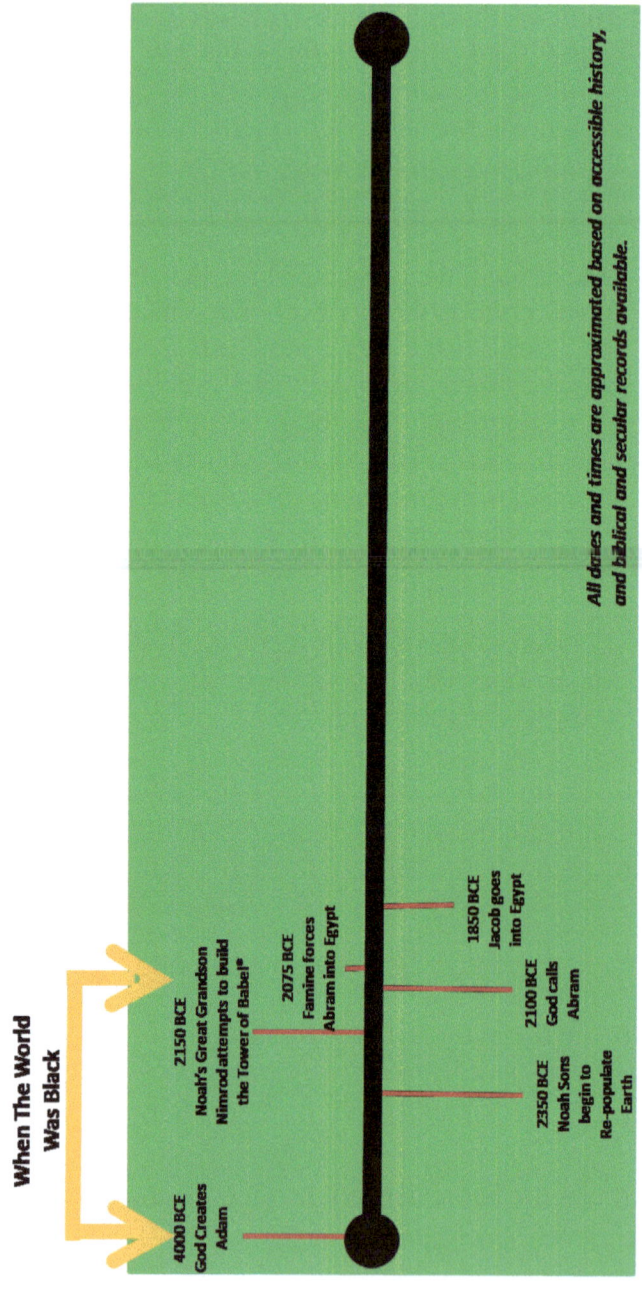

When The World Was Black

4000 BCE God Creates Adam

2350 BCE Noah Sons begin to Re-populate Earth

2150 BCE Noah's Great Grandson Nimrod attempts to build the Tower of Babel"

2100 BCE God calls Abram

2075 BCE Famine forces Abram into Egypt

1850 BCE Jacob goes into Egypt

All dates and times are approximated based on accessible history, and biblical and secular records available.

MOSES MARRIES AND ETHIOPIAN

This entry into our timeline occurs at approximately 1420 BCE.

This Black History encounter is referenced in Numbers chapter 12, verse 1. It reads"

> *"Then Miriam and Aaron spoke against Moses because of the Cushite woman whom he had married (for he had married a Cushite woman);"*
>
> **Numbers 12:1**

Just when Moses married the Cushite wife is the subject of much debate. We are told in Exodus chapter 3 that Moses' wife was a Midianite.[44]but later in the above referenced scripture, we see that he has a Cushite wife. This has long been the source of much discussion and debate. Did Moses divorce and marry a second wife? After all, it was he who created the divorce decree that enabled the children of Israel to get rid of one wife and marry another.[45]We don't have ample history of the nations at this time, so it very well may be that the Midianites were themselves Cushites. But whether she was Moses' only wife or his second wife, she was black! And she stood with him as God used him to lead the children of Israel out of Egypt.

And this was a Black History Moment for the annuls of time. Moses, God's deliverer, marries an African Cushite and the rest is history!

---

[44] Exodus 3:1
[45] Matthew 19:7-9

Biblical/Historical Timeline

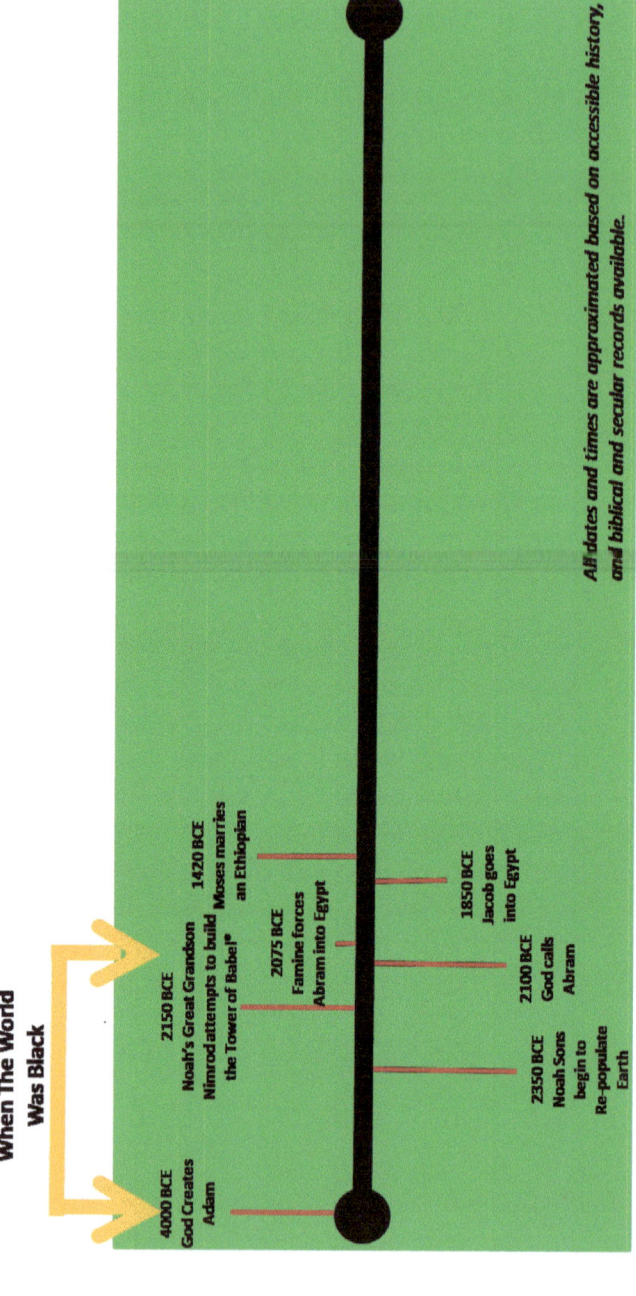

When The World Was Black

4000 BCE
God Creates Adam

2350 BCE
Noah Sons begin to Re-populate Earth

2150 BCE
Noah's Great Grandson Nimrod attempts to build the Tower of Babel"

2100 BCE
God calls Abram

2075 BCE
Famine forces Abram into Egypt

1850 BCE
Jacob goes into Egypt

1420 BCE
Moses marries an Ethiopian

All dates and times are approximated based on accessible history, and biblical and secular records available.

THE QUEEN OF SHEBA VISITS SOLOMON

This entry into our timeline occurs at approximately 980 BCE.

This Black History encounter is recorded in the tenth chapter of First Kings.

Solomon has risen to the throne in Jerusalem and his wisdom is legendary within local circles. As the King of Israel, his legendary reputation would not have reached global heights at this time, so God sends Queen Makeda, the queen of Sheba in biblical Ethiopia, up to Jerusalem. Queen Makeda is already established as a highly esteemed world leader, so any endorsement or approval from her would be far reaching in establishing Solomon's reputation globally. It appears that God is using Queen Makeda to establish Solomon's reputation globally. She had heard of the Wisdom of Solomon, but she wanted to see for herself before proclaiming his greatness to the world. She then travels up to Jerusalem, bringing many precious and valuable gifts with her, and first gives Solomon a test of hard questions. When Solomon correctly answered her questions, she observed his house and took note of everything about him; she then proclaimed that what she had heard of him was true and she announced to the world that of the news concerning Solomon and his wisdom, the half wasn't even being told.

In the history of modern-day Ethiopia, it is said that Queen Makeda and Solomon had a son who established the Solomonic dynasty in Ethiopia.[46]

Regardless of how you wish to view this history, this is a relevant Black History Moment. An Ethiopian queen of

---

[46] Dictionary of African Christian Biography --
https://dacb.org/stories/ethiopia/makeda/

great statue comes to Jerusalem, gives the King of Israel a test, and upon successful completion of the test, she gives him her approval and endorses him to the world.

Furthermore, she is preserved in the annals of The Faith as Jesus himself proclaimed that her example of travelling such a distance just to examine the wisdom of Solomon would be used against the people of His day who wouldn't even expend a very little effort to come and experience God.

The Queen Makeda Black History event should be announced from the mountaintops and her example of power, grace, beauty, and governance should be held as an example of the heights every little Black girl can attain.

Biblical/Historical Timeline

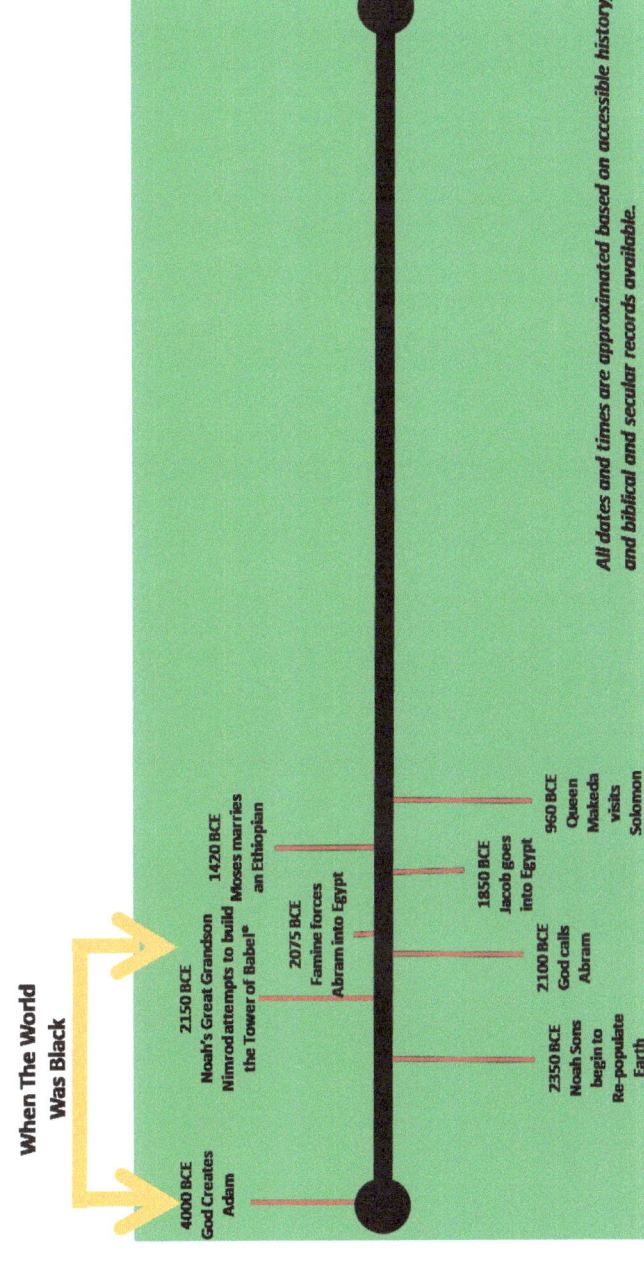

When The World Was Black

4000 BCE
God Creates
Adam

2350 BCE
Noah Sons
begin to
Re-populate
Earth

2150 BCE
Noah's Great Grandson
Nimrod attempts to build
the Tower of Babel"

2100 BCE
God calls
Abram

2075 BCE
Famine forces
Abram into Egypt

1850 BCE
Jacob goes
into Egypt

1420 BCE
Moses marries
an Ethiopian

960 BCE
Queen
Makeda
visits
Solomon

All dates and times are approximated based on accessible history, and biblical and secular records available.

ZERA THE ETHIOPIAN MAKES
WAR WITH JUDAH

This entry into our timeline occurs at approximately 870 BCE.

This Black History encounter is recorded in the fourteenth chapter of Second Chronicles.

Not all the interactions between Israel and the descendants of Ham are pleasurable. In this particular instance, Zera, the powerful king of Ethiopia, invades Judah at the time when Asa was king. So powerful and mighty was Zera, that the scriptures says that he came out against Asa with an army of one million soldiers and three hundred chariots. But Zera was on the wrong side in this fight. Asa was a king that did right in the sight of God, so when he called upon the God, God came to his rescue and put down Zera. But the size of his army indicates his might and power. It tells the story of a biblical Ethiopia where there was great wealth, great might, and great power. When Asa called upon God for help, he emphasized the great might of the Ethiopians and their inability to defeat them without divine intervention.

Although God had to put him down, Zera continued the long line of powerful black African leaders.

Biblical/Historical Timeline

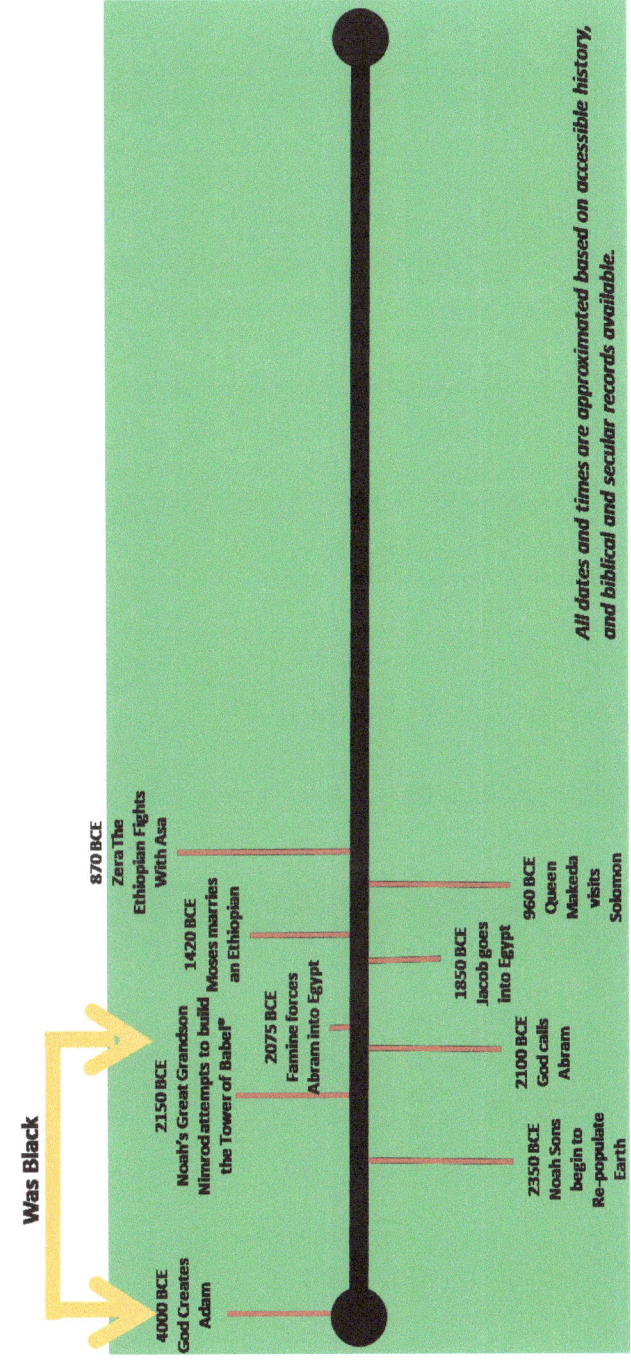

Was Black

4000 BCE
God Creates
Adam

2350 BCE
Noah Sons
begin to
Re-populate
Earth

2150 BCE
Noah's Great Grandson
Nimrod attempts to build
the Tower of Babel"

2100 BCE
God calls
Abram

2075 BCE
Famine forces
Abram into Egypt

1850 BCE
Jacob goes
into Egypt

1420 BCE
Moses marries
an Ethiopian

960 BCE
Queen
Makeda
visits
Solomon

870 BCE
Zera The
Ethiopian Fights
With Asa

*All dates and times are approximated based on accessible history,
and biblical and secular records available.*

KING TIRHAKAH SAVES ISRAEL

This entry into our timeline occurs at approximately 675 BCE.

This Black History encounter is recorded in the nineteenth chapter of Second Kings.

This is one of the first battles for Jerusalem where God intervenes and destroys the army of Assyria. The Lord causes a rumor to be circulated amongst the Assyrians that the powerful king Tirhakah, who ruled over Ethiopia, and his Ethiopian army, were advancing toward Assyria.

The Ethiopian King Tirhakah was so powerful that the mere mention of his name created fear in the hearts of those that would oppose him.

The history surrounding Tirhakah is well documented in the annals of archaeology. He is mentioned two times in the Bible.

Biblical/Historical Timeline

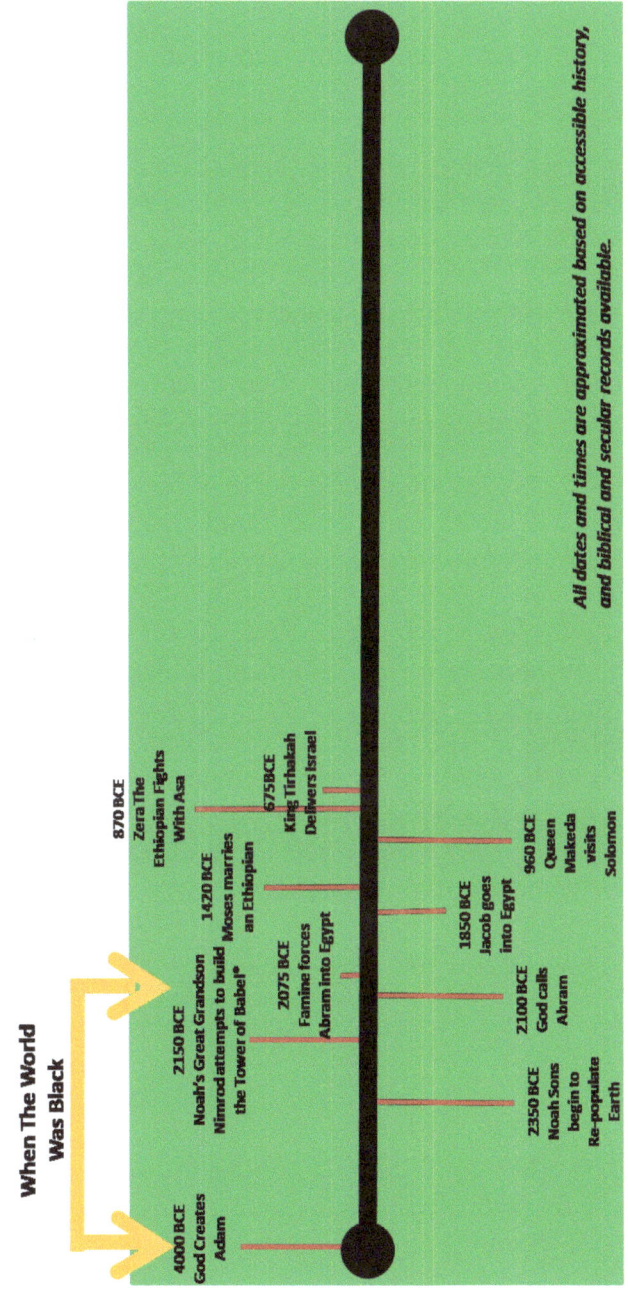

When The World Was Black

4000 BCE God Creates Adam

2350 BCE Noah Sons begin to Re-populate Earth

2150 BCE Noah's Great Grandson Nimrod attempts to build the Tower of Babel*

2100 BCE God calls Abram

2075 BCE Famine forces Abram into Egypt

1850 BCE Jacob goes into Egypt

1420 BCE Moses marries an Ethiopian

960 BCE Queen Makeda visits Solomon

870 BCE Zera The Ethiopian Fights With Asa

675BCE King Tirhakah Delivers Israel

All dates and times are approximated based on accessible history, and biblical and secular records available.

EBED-MELECH SAVES THE
PROPHET JEREMIAH

This entry into our timeline occurs at approximately 586 BCE.

This Black History encounter is recorded in the thirty-eighth chapter of Jeremiah.

Jeremiah, a famous prophet of God to his people, was charged with delivering some very unpopular news. As is often the case with those who deliver truth and it is not good, Jeremiah wasn't very popular in the kingdom. King Zedekiah's advisors convinced him that Jeremiah needed to be put to death. The king agreed because he too, was angry about Jeremiah's prophecy. So, the king's advisors took Jeremiah and lowered him down into a well to die. No trial, no judge, no jury, and no explanation of charges. They took matters in their own hands.

But, Ebed-Melech, an Ethiopian Eunuch, heard of the injustice done to Jeremiah and he petitions the king for the prophet's life. The king says, "Do whatever you want." So, Ebed-Melech got the 30 men recommended by the king to help him rescue Jeremiah from the muddy well. These men, being led by the Ethiopian Ebed-Melech, pulled Jeremiah up from the mud and certain death.

God was pleased with Ebed-Melech's work.

Biblical/Historical Timeline

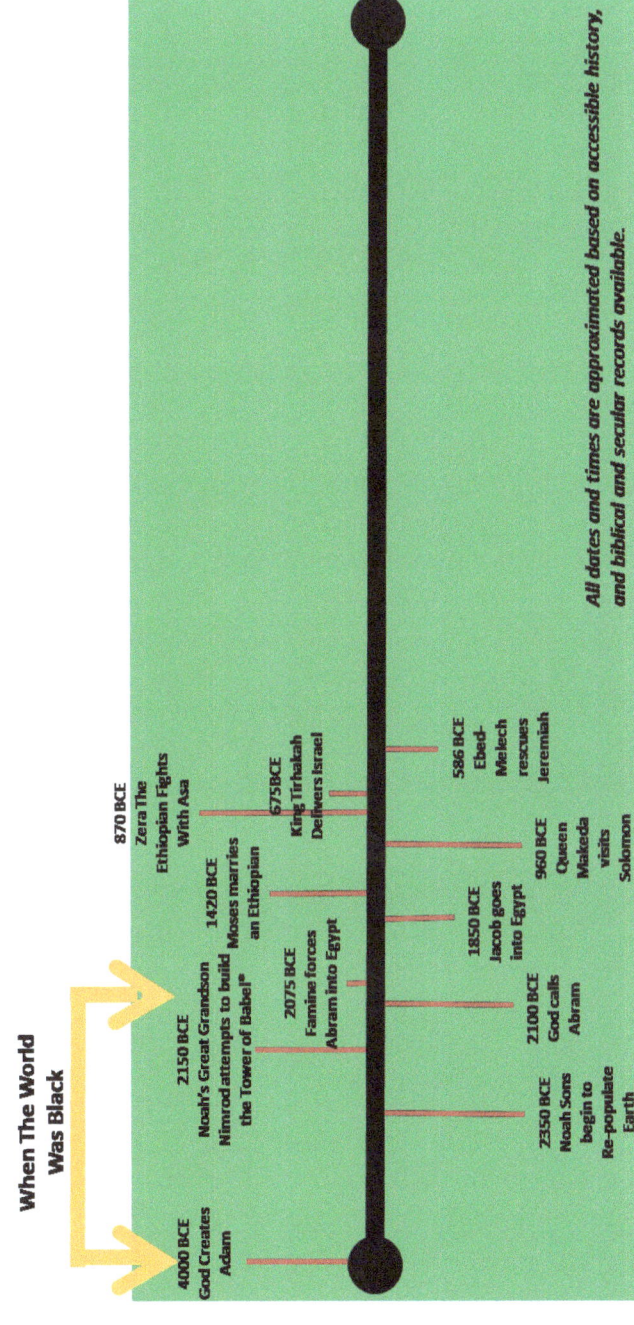

When The World Was Black

4000 BCE
God Creates Adam

2350 BCE
Noah Sons begin to Re-populate Earth

2150 BCE
Noah's Great Grandson Nimrod attempts to build the Tower of Babel"

2100 BCE
God calls Abram

2075 BCE
Famine forces Abram into Egypt

1850 BCE
Jacob goes into Egypt

1420 BCE
Moses marries an Ethiopian

960 BCE
Queen Makeda visits Solomon

870 BCE
Zera The Ethiopian Fights With Asa

675BCE
King Tirhakah Delivers Israel

586 BCE
Ebed-Melech rescues Jeremiah

All dates and times are approximated based on accessible history, and biblical and secular records available.

BIRTH OF JESUS/JESUS IS TAKEN INTO EGYPT

This entry into our timeline occurs at approximately 0 BCE/0 CE.

These Black History encounters are recorded in the second chapter of Luke.

So we now come to the birth of Jesus. This is a black history moment indeed. Jesus is a descendant of the African Sumerian, Abraham. He has come into this world as a man to advocate, intercede, and mediate for us as the Priest for the world. Because of Him, every man, woman, boy, and girl will have access to God.

But immediately after Jesus' birth, King Herod seeks to kill Him. And once again, God directs him to safety in the land of Ham. Just as Egypt did for Abraham and Jacob, Egypt (Ham's son Mizraim) now provides a safe haven for our Lord and savior. Egypt, an African nation, provides for Israel just as it has always done. This showcases the enormous responsibility that God entrusted to Africa and Africans.

This is Black History!

And for the records, Revelation 1:14-15 provides a vivid description of Jesus, describing Him as a man with brown skin, the color of burnished brass. No doubt he had many of the physical characteristics of his African Sumerian ancestor, Abraham.

Biblical/Historical Timeline

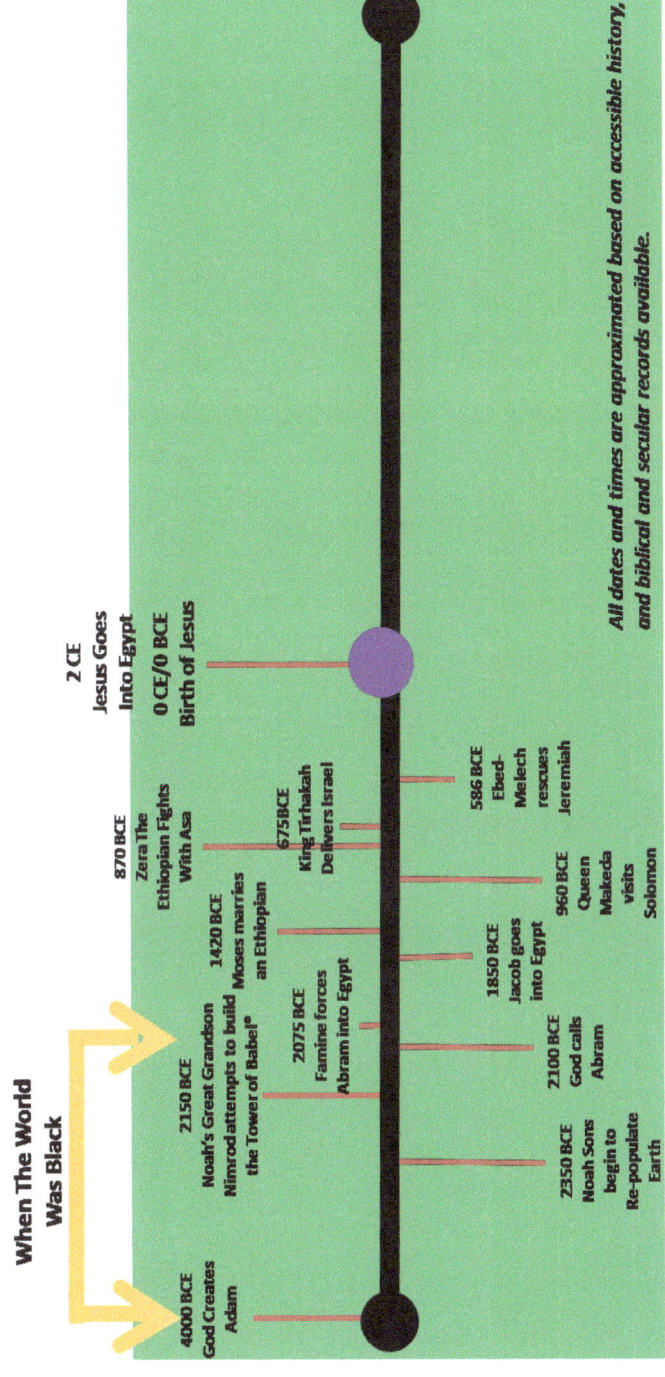

When The World Was Black

4000 BCE
God Creates Adam

2350 BCE
Noah Sons begin to Re-populate Earth

2150 BCE
Noah's Great Grandson Nimrod attempts to build the Tower of Babel"

2075 BCE
Famine forces Abram into Egypt

2100 BCE
God calls Abram

1850 BCE
Jacob goes into Egypt

1420 BCE
Moses marries an Ethiopian

870 BCE
Zera The Ethiopian Fights With Asa

960 BCE
Queen Makeda visits Solomon

675BCE
King Tirhakah Delivers Israel

585 BCE
Ebed-Melech rescues Jeremiah

2 CE
Jesus Goes Into Egypt

0 CE/0 BCE
Birth of Jesus

All dates and times are approximated based on accessible history, and biblical and secular records available.

SIMON OF CYRENE HELPS JESUS

This entry into our timeline occurs at approximately 33 CE.

This Black History encounter is recorded in the fifteenth chapter of Mark.

If ever an incident served as a portrayal of the relationship that God purposed for the Africans and the Jews, this is it. We have seen the Africans aid Israel in the time of famine; we've seen the Africans come to the aid of Israel in the times of war; we've seen the Africans place their life on the line to save the life of the Prophet; but no other incident reveals God plan for the descendants of Ham as this.

Our Lord and Savior has been unjustly sentenced to death by crucifixion. He has been beaten bloody to the point of near death. And in a weakened state, He has the weight of the cross slammed on his back and is told to carry it to Calvary's Hill. He's being spit on, whipped, laughed at, and mocked as he attempts carry the cross. But God has His help in place. For when Jesus was unable to carry the cross, the Roman guards looked over the crowd and their eyes fell on Simon of Cyrene. The Romans may have thought that they were exercising dominion over this African, but in reality it was God who had placed Simon at the right place and at the right time for his assignment. Simon took the cross of our Lord and Savior and carried it up to Calvary.

In this Black History moment, we see the responsibility that God has bestowed on the African descendants of Ham, for even in the darkest hour of Jesus' life as a man, God selected an African to be there for him. AND BE THERE FOR HIM HE WAS!

Biblical/Historical Timeline

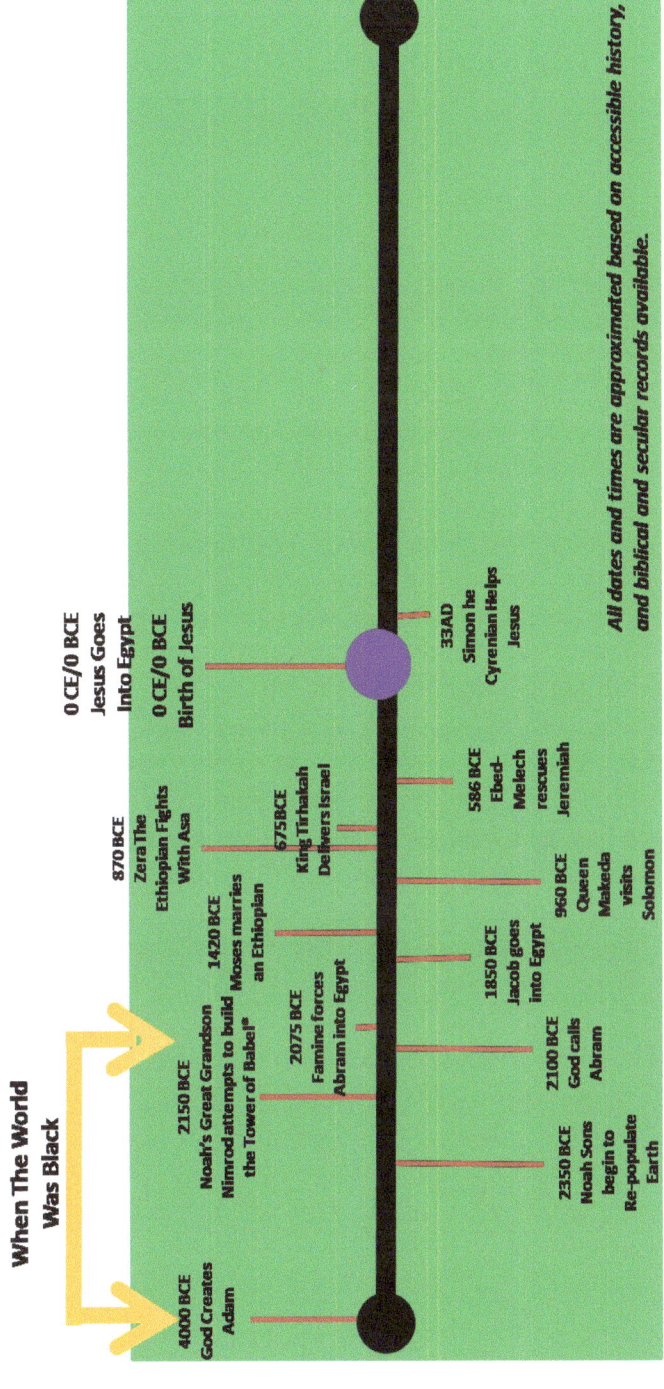

When The World Was Black

4000 BCE
God Creates Adam

2350 BCE
Noah Sons begin to Re-populate Earth

2150 BCE
Noah's Great Grandson Nimrod attempts to build the Tower of Babel"

2075 BCE
Famine forces Abram into Egypt

2100 BCE
God calls Abram

1850 BCE
Jacob goes into Egypt

1420 BCE
Moses marries an Ethiopian

960 BCE
Queen Makeda visits Solomon

870 BCE
Zera The Ethiopian Fights With Asa

675BCE
King Tirhakah Delivers Israel

586 BCE
Ebed-Melech rescues Jeremiah

0 CE/0 BCE
Jesus Goes Into Egypt

0 CE/0 BCE
Birth of Jesus

33AD
Simon he Cyrenian Helps Jesus

All dates and times are approximated based on accessible history, and biblical and secular records available.

THE ETHIOPIAN EUNUCH CARRIES THE FAITH BACK TO AFRICA

This entry into our timeline occurs at approximately 33-69 CE.

This Black History encounter is recorded in the eighth chapter of Acts.

At this point, The Faith is growing rapidly and immensely among the Jews. Paul, known at the time as Saul, hasn't come into the Believer's fold as of yet. He was persecuting Believers. But this persecution served as a catalyst for the growth of The Faith. Phillip was preaching in the towns and villages. One day, as he was heading back to Jerusalem, God spoke to him and told him to go another way. As he travelled the other way, he saw a chariot and God told him to approach it. When he approached the chariot, he saw an Ethiopian sitting, reading scripture and trying to gain understanding. This Ethiopian was a servant of the powerful Ethiopian Queen Candace. Phillip then explained to him what he was reading and how this particular scripture was speaking of Jesus. Phillip's explanation of scripture allowed him to preach salvation through Jesus and even baptize the Ethiopian. Immediately after this encounter, Phillip was carried away to another place by the Holy Spirit.

This Black History encounter reveals that The Faith made it to Africa even before it made it to many of the Gentile nations.

Biblical/Historical Timeline

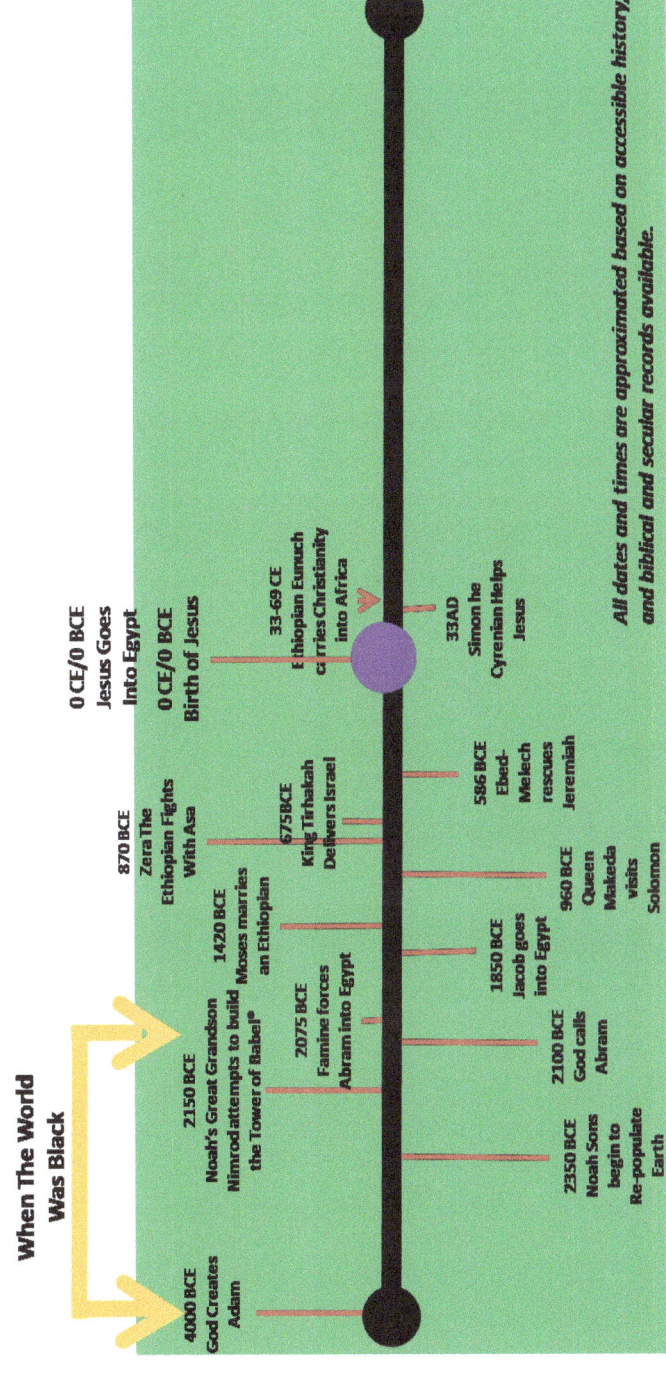

When The World Was Black

4000 BCE God Creates Adam

2350 BCE Noah Sons begin to Re-populate Earth

2150 BCE Noah's Great Grandson Nimrod attempts to build the Tower of Babel®

2100 BCE God calls Abram

2075 BCE Famine forces Abram into Egypt

1850 BCE Jacob goes into Egypt

1420 BCE Moses marries an Ethiopian

960 BCE Queen Makeda visits Solomon

870 BCE Zera The Ethiopian Fights With Asa

675 BCE King Tirhakah Delivers Israel

586 BCE Ebed-Melech rescues Jeremiah

0 CE/0 BCE Jesus Goes Into Egypt

0 CE/0 BCE Birth of Jesus

33-69 CE Ethiopian Eunuch carries Christianity into Africa

33AD Simon he Cyrenian Helps Jesus

All dates and times are approximated based on accessible history, and biblical and secular records available.

89

BARNABAS, SIMEON WHO WAS CALLED NIGER, LUCIUS OF CYRENE, -- BLACK PROPHETS OF THE EARLY CHURCH

This entry into our timeline occurs at approximately 33 -69 CE.

These Black History encounters are recorded in the thirteenth chapter of Acts.

For this Black History event, I will not create an entry on the timeline because this occurs at about the time that Phillip encounters the Ethiopian. But the fact that this is divinely inspired scripture illustrates the point that Jesus made to the Jews when He walked the earth. In John chapter 10, verse 16 Jesus tells the Jews:

> *"And I have other sheep that are not of this fold; I must bring them also, and they will listen to My voice; and they will become one flock, with one shepherd."*
>
> **John 10:16**

We know that sheep represents people in this verse, and the fold is the Jews. So Jesus is telling the Jews that He has other people that are not Jews, and He must gather them also because the objective is to have one flock, regardless of which fold (nationality) the sheep are from.

So in the early church we see Simeon, who is call Niger, Lucius of Cyrene, and Barnabas where some of the "*other sheep*" that Jesus referred to. They were among the prophets and teachers who displayed character that so closely matched Jesus, they became the reason that outsiders begin referring to Believers as 'Christians'.

Lucius is identified as being from Cyrene, a city in Libya, North Africa. Therefore, we know that he is African, or Black. Simeon is one that is referred to a Niger. The word Niger is translated as 'Black', thereby indicating that Simeon was indeed a Black man from Africa; and that he was fervent in preaching, prophesying, and teaching the Gospel. He is presumed to be an African who had relocated to Antioch and met with Jesus. Some scholars hold that he is the same Simon of Cyrene that carried the cross of Jesus, but the spelling of the name is different. They mainly arrive at this conclusion because He is associated with Lucuis, who is from Cyrene, just as Simon the cross bearer was. Simeon's appearance here in the book of Acts does not indicate his nationality or ethnic origin. It simply indicates that he is called 'Niger', or black. The Bible indicates that Barnabas was a Levite that was born in Northern Africa.[47] The fact that Barnabas was a Levite that was born in Africa validates and verifies the relevance of God's relationship with Black people. It shows that Israel is Africa, and it is a powerful endorsement of the Jews being people of color, or Northern African Black. So in these three Black Men of God, we see two black descendants of Ham, and one Black Descendant of Shem.

But the Black History Moment to behold here is the beauty of having divinely inspired scripture that shows how Black People played a fundamental role in the beginnings of the early church.

---

[47] Acts 4:36

THE NEW TESTAMENT IS AUTHENTICATED (CANONIZED) IN NORTH AFRICA

This entry into our timeline occurs at approximately 393 & 397 CE.

The twenty-seven books of the New Testament were first formally canonized during the councils of Hippo (393 A.D.) and Carthage (397 A.D.) in North Africa.

This Black History moment further illustrates God's relationship with the African people and the enormous responsibility that he has placed with Africans and people of African Ancestry.

Biblical/Historical Timeline

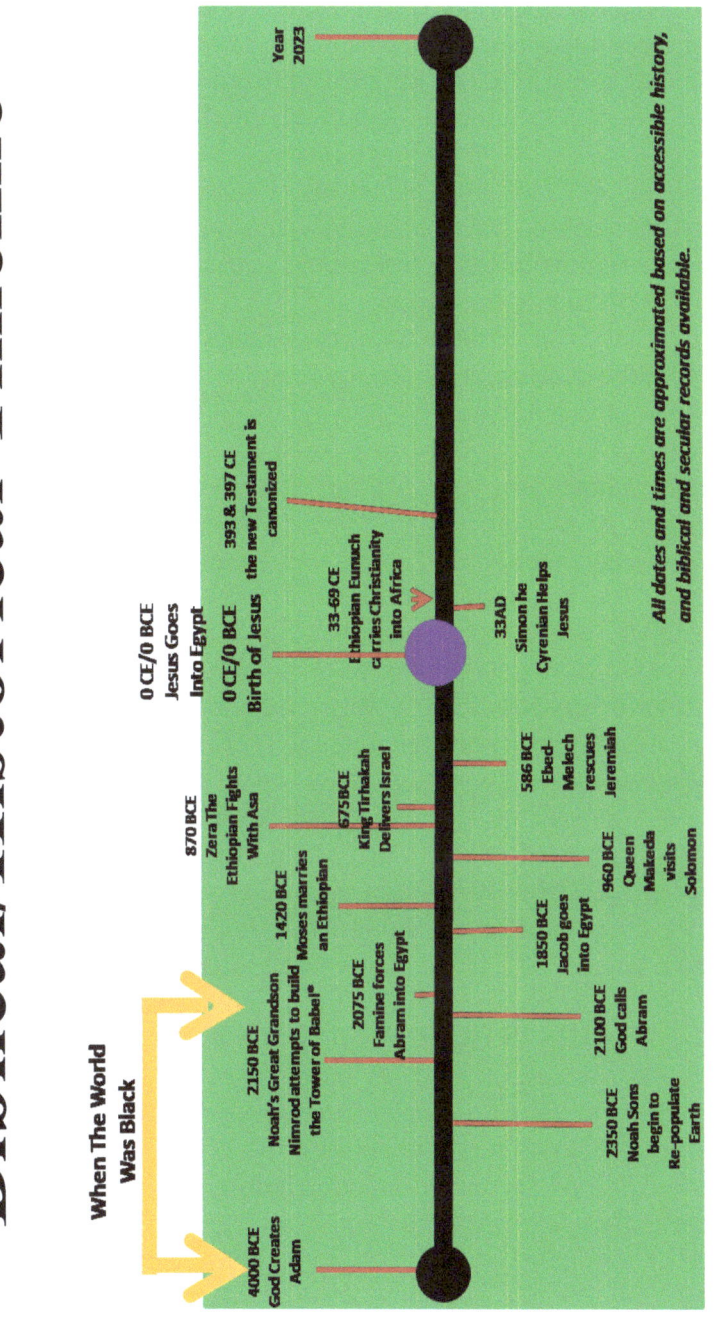

When The World Was Black

4000 BCE
God Creates Adam

2350 BCE
Noah Sons begin to Re-populate Earth

2150 BCE
Noah's Great Grandson Nimrod attempts to build the Tower of Babel®

2100 BCE
God calls Abram

2075 BCE
Famine forces Abram into Egypt

1850 BCE
Jacob goes into Egypt

1420 BCE
Moses marries an Ethiopian

960 BCE
Queen Makeda visits Solomon

870 BCE
Zera The Ethiopian Fights With Asa

675BCE
King Tirhakah Delivers Israel

586 BCE
Ebed-Melech rescues Jeremiah

0 CE/0 BCE
Jesus Goes Into Egypt

0 CE/0 BCE
Birth of Jesus

33-69 CE
Ethiopian Eunuch carries Christianity into Africa

33AD
Simon he Cyrenian Helps Jesus

393 & 397 CE
the new Testament is canonized

Year 2023

All dates and times are approximated based on accessible history, and biblical and secular records available.

This concludes the biblical interactions that the Jews had with Ham's descendant of which I will cover in this book. The objective was to call out the major interactions between these two nations after Abraham was sent to Canaan.

I did this because after Abraham is sent to Canaan, the scriptures focuses solely on the Jewish people because their divine assignment was to receive the instructions from God, apply them first to themselves, and then teach the world the ways of God. So the only times that Ham's descendants are written about in scripture are the times that they interacted with the Jewish people.

These interactions with the Jewish people reveal one pertinent point. God established the Africans with wealth beyond imagination; He then graced them with power and might. You'll notice that Israel did not have a single encounter with a weak, poor, or disgraced African. And every time God called upon the Africans, they were there. Whether it was providing food in a famine, safety in a time of trouble, military power and might in times of war, or just courage to stand up for the Jews when they were being unjustly persecuted. The African descendants of Ham always answered when God called. In my book, The Children of The Ethiopians, I show that when doing this, Ham's descendants were doing what God selected them to do as a nation, just like Israel was selected to serve as Priests.

THIS IS REAL BLACK HISTORY!

I will now display my final Timeline. I have added only a couple of additional points because when I teach this as a class, these points are discussion points that provide an opportunity to explain even more Black History.

Biblical/Historical Timeline

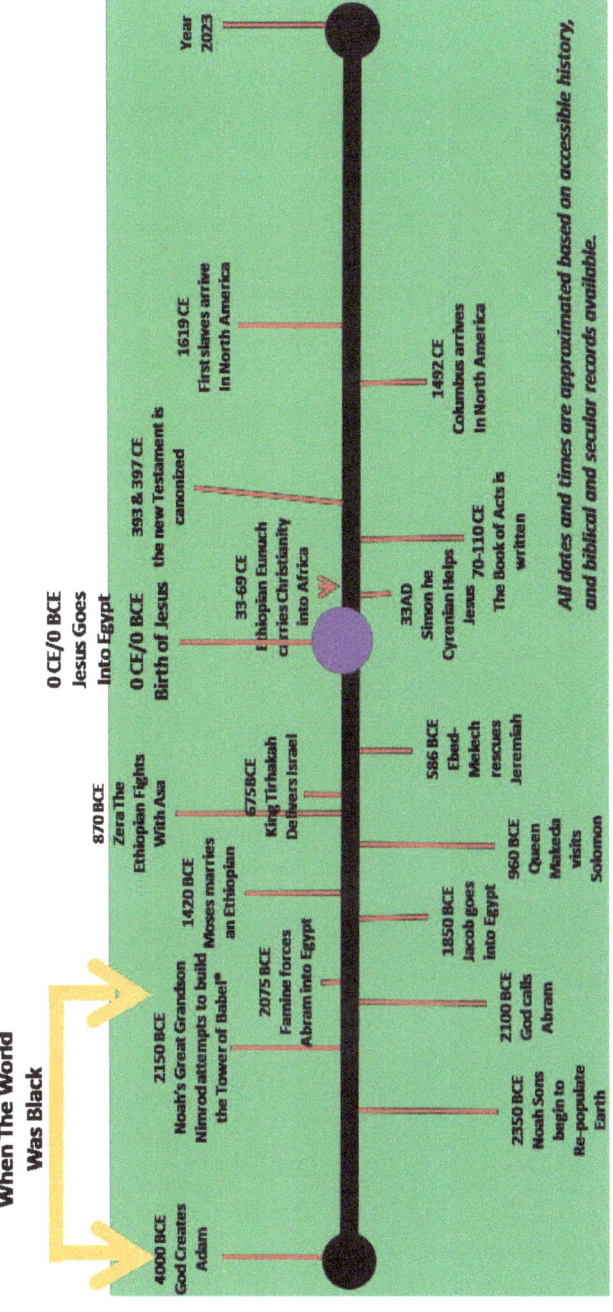

When The World
Was Black

4000 BCE
God Creates
Adam

2350 BCE
Noah Sons
begin to
Re-populate
Earth

2150 BCE
Noah's Great Grandson
Nimrod attempts to build
the Tower of Babel"

2075 BCE
Famine forces
Abram into Egypt

2100 BCE
God calls
Abram

1850 BCE
Jacob goes
into Egypt

1420 BCE
Moses marries
an Ethiopian

960 BCE
Queen
Makeda
visits
Solomon

870 BCE
Zera The
Ethiopian Fights
With Asa

675 BCE
King Tirhakah
Delivers Israel

586 BCE
Ebed-
Melech
rescues
Jeremiah

0 CE/0 BCE
Jesus Goes
Into Egypt

0 CE/0 BCE
Birth of Jesus

33-69 CE
Ethiopian Eunuch
carries Christianity
into Africa

33AD
Simon he
Cyrenian Helps
Jesus

70-110 CE
The Book of Acts is
written

393 & 397 CE
the new Testament is
canonized

1492 CE
Columbus arrives
In North America

1619 CE
First slaves arrive
In North America

Year
2023

*All dates and times are approximated based on accessible history,
and biblical and secular records available.*

All of Ham's descendants were prosperous people with enormous influence throughout the world. The Bible even lets us know that places were blessed simply because Ham's descendants lived there.

> "39. And they went to the entrance of Gedor, even unto the east side of the valley, to seek pasture for their flocks.
> 40. And they found fat pasture and good, and the land was wide, and quiet, and peaceable; for they of Ham had dwelt there of old."
> **1 Chronicles 4:39-40**

These blessings upon the descendants of Ham throughout the Bible are a direct result of their spirituality and their relationship with God. Much has been said and written about the spirituality of biblical Africans, but truth being told, the bible indicates that biblical Africans were very committed to God and very spiritual people; they only worshipped the true and living God, even when they only knew of Him as a Supreme Being.

The next chapter of this book will briefly examine and analyze the spirituality of Africans throughout history. In this chapter, many myths, non-truths, and outright lies will be dispelled.

GOD'S GOVERNANCE *and* BLACK SPIRITUALITY

"For since the creation of the world His invisible attributes,
that is, His eternal power and divine nature, have been
clearly perceived, being understood by what has been
made, so that they are without excuse."

Romans 1:20.

Much has been written about the spirituality of early
Africans and their descendants. And much of this written
material represents the work of those who colluded to

dehumanize African people, dismiss their relationship with God, and steal the valuable resources that God placed under their control. So the first thing to consider in discussions about African Spirituality is the source. Many of the documents used as sources were created to promote the narrative of Africans being 'uncivilized beasts' who needed to have Christianity presented to them. This narrative fit two bills for the Western Christian evangelists:

1. It validated, in their minds, that they were obeying scripture by preaching the Gospel to the *'creature'*.*

2. It justified the seizing of the African lands and the valuable resources that God placed there. (**Colonization**)

But when we look accurately at the spirituality of indigenous Africans, you see that the narrative of uncivilized idol worshippers is far from true.

Let's Take a Look!

To examine Black Spirituality, we must first re-visit our timeline and make it relative to God's governance. When studying the bible, it is imperative that we understand the ways that God governed his creation from the very beginning; from the creation of Adam. So I'll give a very brief overview of God's governance of man since creation.

GOD'S GOVERNANCE OF MAN
THROUGHOUT THE AGES

We know from Bible study that God has governed his creation in four distinct ways since the creation of Adam.

1. This was the period of individual direct governance via the soul of man. This was the time period that preceded the law and spanned from Adam to Moses. During this period of governance, God gave instructions, and made His desires and His will known to each individual man. This relationship between God and man was made possible by the creation of man as a 'living soul'. The soul of man being from God, belonging to God, and having direct access to God, just as a child has to a parent, allows for a direct relationship with God. Being created as living souls, man enjoys citizenship in two distinct worlds. Our body is us in the Physical Natural World, whereas our Soul is us in the Spiritual Supernatural World; hence the allowance of a direct relationship with God via our soul. During this period of Governance, only God would know when man violated His will with their actions, because there were no universally documented requirements from God. The Apostle Paul put it this way in Romans 5:13

> *"for until the Law sin was in the world, but sin is not counted against anyone when there is no law.."*
>
> **Romans 5:13**

Paul emphasizes that because there was no open universally applied requirement, one could not be charged with violating the requirement, since the requirement was not known or did not exist. But we know that many did not meet God's requirement during this time, [48]and they were appropriately disciplined by God for their disobedience. This God did justly because each individual is a 'living soul'. And therewith, a method of direct communication with God exists, and it is inherent with man since creaton.

---

[48] Genesis 6:10

2. The second period of God's governance of man was via the law. God commenced giving laws to govern man with Moses. This period of governance spanned in time from the giving of the law until God gave Israel prophets, or from Moses until Samuel.

"For the Law was given through Moses;…"

John 1:17

But just as important as it is to understand that the law was given to apply God's governance to humanity, it is equally important to understand to whom the law was given and the reasons for which it was given. It is critical to understand that **the law was given to Israel!** This is a crucial point in explaining the spirituality of any nation because it was Israel's assignment as the priests of the earth to first learn these laws of God, apply these laws to themselves, then teach them to the other nations of the world.[49] So, until Israel functioned in their calling as priests, the other nations remained under God's individual direct governance via the soul, simply because the law, which was to be delivered and taught to them by Israel, had not made it to them because of Israel's constant failure. Jesus would be the remedy for this failure but He would not appear on the scene until some 1500 years after the law was given to Moses.

THIS IS WHY THE PERFECTION OF JESUS IS THE FOUNDATION FOR SALVATION. HE DID, AS AN ISRAELITE, WHAT ISRAEL FAILED TO DO AS A NATION. This will be further examined in the fourth method of God's governance.

3. The third period of God's governance of man was via the prophets. Many people include the prophets in God's

---

[49] Exodus 19:5-6, Deuteronomy 7:6-7

governance via the law, but Jesus and the Apostle Paul were careful to make distinction between the Law and the Prophets.

> "*The Law and the Prophets were proclaimed until John came*"
> **Luke 16:16**

> "*Do not presume that I came to abolish the Law or the prophets; I did not come to abolish, but to fulfill*"
> **Matthew 5:17**

> "*But now the righteousness of God without the law is manifested, being witnessed by the law and the prophets;*"
> **Romans 3:21**

This third period of God's governance via the prophets spanned from Samuel until Jesus. (*Actually, this governance period ended at Malachi because there was no open word from God for 400 years prior to the birth of Jesus.*) It should also be noted that the prophets were <u>sent to Israel</u> because they failed to learn and keep the law themselves, hence they could never teach this law to the other nations. Therefore the prophets were sent to provide guidance and correction.

"Yet He sent prophets to them to bring them back to the Lord; and they testified against them, but they would not listen."

2 Chronicles 24:19

"Also I have sent to you all My servants the prophets, sending them again and again, saying: 'Turn now every person from his evil way and amend your deeds, and do not follow other gods to worship them. Then you will live in the land which I have given to you and to your forefathers; but you have not inclined your ear or listened to Me."

Jeremiah 35:15

It should too be noted before we present the fourth method of God's governance, that each method is cumulative in that the succeeding method of governance was added to the commands and instructions that God gave in the previous method of governance. Hence, the law did not negate any command or instruction that God had given directly, it was in addition to and strengthened those instructions. Likewise, the prophets did not cancel or negate the law, but any instructions from God via the prophets to the people strengthened and were in addition to the instructions contained in the law. The fourth method of God's governance continued this governance process.

4. The fourth period of God's governance of man is the period of grace that came via Jesus. This period, which we commonly call grace, is the period in which God dwells in man. The Bible refers to this period as "The Kingdom of God." In this period, God would place His spirit in man and empower man to fulfill the instructions given in the law and the prophets. This period started with John the Baptist.

"The Law and the Prophets were proclaimed until John came; since that time the gospel of the kingdom of God has been preached, and everyone is forcing his way into it."

Luke 16:16

This is the period of God's governance that we are currently in and it will continue until Jesus second coming.

Let's add these governance periods to our timeline.

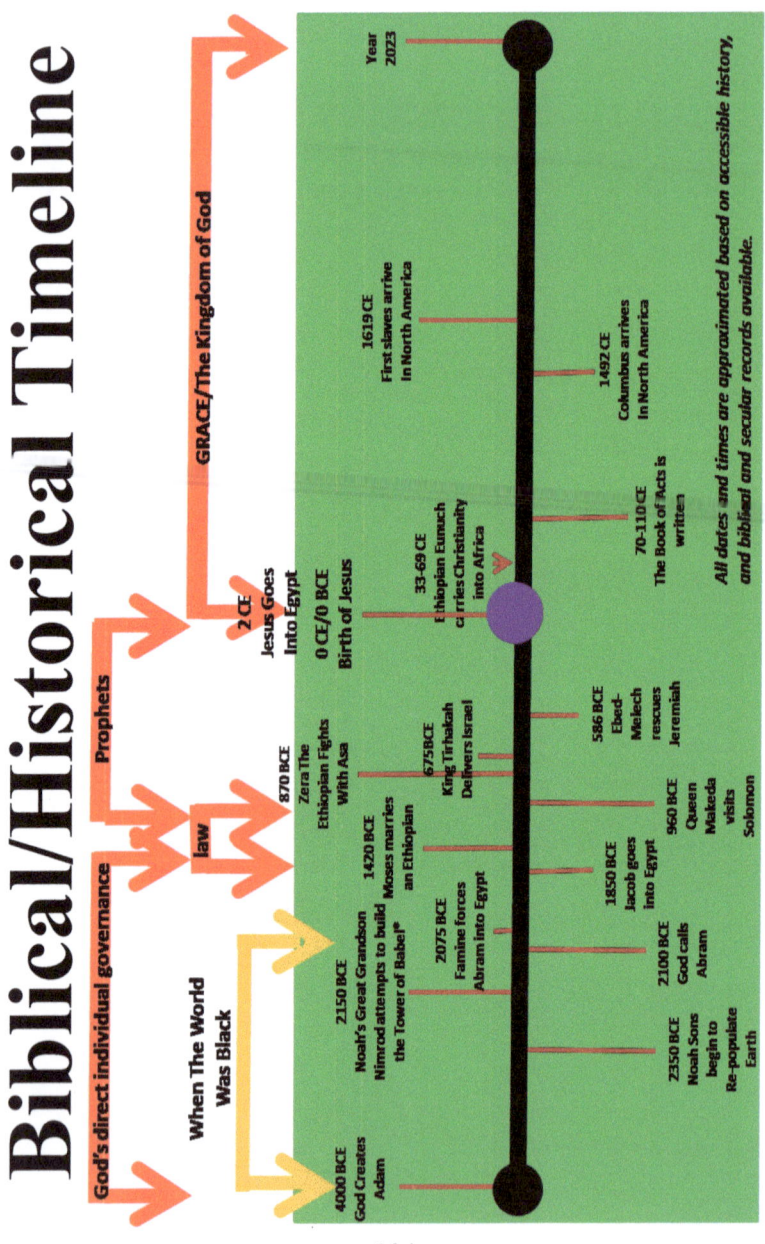

Biblical/Historical Timeline

God's direct individual governance

law

Prophets

GRACE/The Kingdom of God

When The World Was Black

4000 BCE
God Creates Adam

2350 BCE
Noah Sons begin to Re-populate Earth

2150 BCE
Noah's Great Grandson Nimrod attempts to build the Tower of Babel*

2100 BCE
God calls Abram

2075 BCE
Famine forces Abram into Egypt

1850 BCE
Jacob goes into Egypt

1420 BCE
Moses marries an Ethiopian

960 BCE
Queen Makeda visits Solomon

870 BCE
Zera The Ethiopian Fights With Asa

675BCE
King Tirhakah Delivers Israel

586 BCE
Ebed-Melech rescues Jeremiah

2 CE
Jesus Goes Into Egypt

0 CE/0 BCE
Birth of Jesus

33-69 CE
Ethiopian Eunuch carries Christianity into Africa

70-110 CE
The Book of Acts is written

1492 CE
Columbus arrives In North America

1619 CE
First slaves arrive In North America

Year 2023

All dates and times are approximated based on accessible history, and biblical and secular records available.

Understanding God's governance is important to African Spirituality because during the pre-law governance period, God had not revealed His requirements universally to mankind, so people only knew of a Supreme Being. However, being created with a soul, they had unctions, urges, and leadings, etc., but they may not have known from whence this guidance emanated. (Moses, being divinely inspired to write about times that preceded him by up to thousands of years, would know at the time of his writing that this direction came from God, but in the moment, the people would not have known. Even Moses said to God at the time that God revealed Himself to him, that the people don't know you.)

> "Then Moses said to God, "Behold, I am going to the sons of Israel, and I will say to them, 'The God of your fathers has sent me to you.' Now they may say to me, 'What is His name?' What shall I say to them?"
>
> **Exodus 3:13**

So in an attempt to give credit to this Supreme Being, the early people created statues of wood, stubble, gold, etc., to represent this Supreme Being. They even attempted to build a tower to where they believe this Supreme Being resided. These were not attempts to reject and replace God, but rather attempts to identify this Supreme Being and show that they understood that they were submissive to Him. Our ancestors were highly intelligent, as I have shown of the African Sumerians. The benefits that they received from the Supreme Being were obvious to them, but they had no knowledge of who this Supreme Being was. If you note, those that they credited as being God were always something or someone greater than they, something that they could not control, and something that they understood provided them with benefit, but just didn't know how to properly credit it. For example, they knew that the Sun was a benefit, they understood that they could not control the sun, and they knew whomever controlled the son was greater than they. So, because of the benefit that they received from the sun, they initiated worship of the sun. Only God would have known whether they were in idolatrous worship, because he had not at the time given the universal instructions of:

"Thou shalt have no other gods before me"

"Thou shalt not make unto thee any graven image, or any likeness of anything that is in heaven above, or that is in the earth beneath, or that is in the water under the earth."

"Thou shalt not bow down thyself to them, nor serve them: for I the Lord thy God am a jealous God,..."

The Apostle Paul said of the people during this time that God overlooked their ignorance.

> *"29. Therefore, since we are the descendants of God, we ought not to think that the Divine Nature is like gold or silver or stone, an image formed by human skill and thought.*
> *30. So having overlooked the times of ignorance, God is now proclaiming to mankind that all people everywhere are to repent,..."*
> **Acts 17:29-30**

But Paul was equally forceful in emphasizing that God no longer overlooks this ignorance but requires all men everywhere to repent.

So prior to knowledge of God's requirements reaching them, our African ancestors and the African Sumerians that emanated from them created these statues and images to express gratitude to the Supreme Being. They were not rejecting God, nor were they attempting to replace God, they were actually showing gratitude to God, the God of whom they had no knowledge.

So looking at our timeline, from Adam to Moses, the descendants of Ham (Africans, African Sumerians, and people of African ancestry) were not idol worshippers, but people attempting to recognize and give credit to a God of whom they had no knowledge. And we can see by the interactions that Israel had with them after Shinar, they mostly followed the urging and unction of the soul and did what was morally, ethically, and socially right. Consider how they interacted with Abraham when he needed rescuing from the Famine; and likewise consider how Pharaoh elevated Joseph and provided food and shelter for his family. We often speak of the bondage of Israel in Africa (Egypt), but we fail to acknowledge that Egypt was the place of their salvation, the place of their nurturing, and the place of their development into a nation.

And even through the governance period of the Law and the Prophets, the descendants of Ham (the Africans, African Sumerians, and those of African ancestry) cannot be charged with worshipping idol gods. The failure of Israel to be the priests meant that Jesus had to come and perform those priestly duties. And we see that the Ethiopian Eunuch of Acts, chapter 8, is the first biblical record of the knowledge of Christ reaching Africa. And until knowledge of Christ reaches any people, they cannot be charged with idolatry for seeking the Supreme Being whose existence they acknowledge, but of whom they have no knowledge. This is why Jesus said that this knowledge must reach everyone before the end can come.

"This gospel of the kingdom shall be preached in the whole world as a testimony to all the nations, and then the end will come."

Matthew 24:14

So, when we understand God's word, we clearly see that the descendants of Ham (Africans, African Sumerians, and those of African ancestry) were NEVER worshippers of idol gods; idol worship was the religious practice that the Apostle Paul identified exclusively with the Gentiles.[50] But it must be emphasized that since Jesus, God's requirement is that all men everywhere repent and accept Jesus.

---

[50] 1 Corinthians 10:20

WHY ALL *of* THIS *is* SO IMPORTANT

"The nations will walk by its light, and the kings of the earth will bring their glory into it."

Revelation 21:24

Whenever I teach on the subject of biblical nations and biblical ethnic origins, I will, without fail, receive one question. This question is inevitably going to pop up, so I am always prepared for it. The question: **Why does this even matter if we are all the same in the eyes of God**? I understand the place from which this question emanates, but my heart sinks with sadness each time I hear it. I am saddened because as Believers, we must accept the words of the Apostle Paul and acknowledge that ALL scripture is inspired by God and should be used for doctrine, correction, rebuke, and training.

"All Scripture is inspired by God and beneficial for teaching, for rebuke, for correction, for training in righteousness."

2 Timothy 3:16

As such, the genealogical tables of Genesis chapter five and the table of nations of Genesis chapter ten and eleven are inspired Holy Scripture. God inspired the writers of scripture to document this for a reason. As a young Believer, whenever I would read Genesis, I would simply skip over these verses and pick up reading after them. But if I had only known then how much of God's plan for the world is contained in these verses, I would have commenced studying and researching them years before I did. Of course, God wanted us to have this knowledge; therefore, He eternalized this knowledge in scripture for anyone willing to understand His plan.

The nations of the world have always been an important part of God's plan for the world. As a matter of fact, you could say that the nations of the world are at the heart of God's plan for the world. It's not that any one nation is more than any other nation in the eyes of God, but each nation has been purposed with individual assignments in God's kingdom on earth. If you recall from scripture, when the disciples asked Jesus to teach them how to pray, the very first request Jesus taught them to make of God was to pray that His kingdom be established here on earth like it is in heaven.

*"Your kingdom come. Your will be done,
On earth as it is in heaven."*

Matthew 6:10

Originally, God's kingdom is in heaven and it is populated with angels that perform His will,[51] but in creating earth and populating it with man, God was expanding His kingdom to earth. In heaven, each angel or order of angels have specific and unique assignments in the kingdom. So if God's kingdom on earth is to be established as it is in heaven, then those that populate the earth will have specific and unique assignments in His kingdom here. I will not go in to detail on this subject in this book because I provided meticulous detail on this in the book **Biblically Black and Blessed II – The Children of The Ethiopians**.

The Bible leaves little doubt in regards to the way in which God purposed to populate His kingdom on earth.

> *"and He made from one man every nation of mankind to live on all the face of the earth,"*
> **Acts 17:26**

He created the nations to populate His kingdom on earth. He is specific that no nation is to oppress, colonize, enslave, or exercise dominion over any other nation.[52] But the nations are to live in a synchronized harmony that makes God's kingdom on earth as peaceful as His kingdom in heaven. In His kingdom on earth, only one nation's kingdom assignment was documented in scripture. And that nation is Israel. They are identified as the people with the assignment of being the Priests to the rest of the world. But we can arrive at the kingdom assignment of the nations that descended from Ham by analyzing their functions when they had interactions with Israel. Ham's descendants were blessed

---

[51] Hebrews 1:13-14, Matthew 26:53, John 1:51
[52] Matthew 20:25-26

people who were rich[53], powerful,[54] smart,[55] moral and ethical;[56] people that provided protection,[57] life sustaining substance,[58] and support[59] at the times that Israel needed help. So we can conclude that the assignment given to the nations that descended from Ham is to be <u>nurturers and mighty protectors of God's righteousness</u>. We have witnessed them functioning in this manner throughout the scripture. I've shown this in this very book. The method used to identify the divine assignment of Ham's descendants is the same method that has been used for centuries to identify the angel Gabriel's assignment in heaven. Scripture declares clearly states that Michael the Archangel's kingdom assignment is to lead an army of angels in heaven,[60] and when he appears in scripture, he is usually fighting wickedness; but we are left to conclude that Gabriel's kingdom assignment is that of a messenger because this is the function that we see him fulfilling throughout scripture.[61] Nowhere in scripture does it say that Gabriel's divine assignment is that of messenger, but whenever he appears in scripture he is carrying a message from God. We therefore conclude that his divine assignment is that of messenger. So we can also conclude that the earthly kingdom assignments given to the nations that descended from Ham are the functions that they fulfilled when they interacted with Israel. To further strengthen our understanding, let's take a look at how God placed the nations.

---

[53] 1 Kings 10,
[54] 2 Chronicles 14:9, 2 Kings 19:9
[55] Acts 8:26-40
[56] Jeremiah 38:6-13
[57] Matthew 2:13-16
[58] Genesis 12:10
[59] Genesis Chapter 46, Mark 15:21-32
[60] Revelation 12:7-9
[61] Luke 1:19, Daniel 9:21, Daniel 8:16

MAP SHOWING ISRAEL'S PLACEMENT
IN THE WORLD

Looking at this map, we see that the center of the world when viewed from this angle is Israel. To the south of Israel, God placed the nations that descended from Ham. To the east of Israel, God placed the nations that descended from Shem. And to the north of Israel, God placed the nations that descended from Japheth. Israel was at the center because it is the place from which God will govern all the nations of His kingdom. In the placement of the nations, God gave all of the nations what they needed to fulfill their kingdom assignment; and He did in a way required that they live together in synchronized harmony.

To Africa and the nations south of Israel, God gave them the vast majority of the world's gold, diamonds, and other precious stones.[62] To the nations east of Israel, God gave

---

[62] Genesis 2:11-12

them the wealth and riches of the world's oil. And to the nations north of Israel, God gave them wealth from land known for its production of grain, and merchant and shipping ports that connect the nations. You can see by the placement of the nations, that God's kingdom on earth required everyone to live in harmony, relying on each other for smooth operations within the overall kingdom. When we view the world from this point, we see Israel's placement as the capital of the world; the place where the King will abide and the place from which He will govern His kingdom.

Now let's move forward to the very end. In Revelation, chapter 21, we see that the heavens and the earth have been replaced by a new heaven and earth.

> "1. Then I saw a new heaven and a new earth; for the first heaven and the first earth passed away, and there is no longer any sea.
> 2. And I saw the holy city, new Jerusalem, coming down out of heaven from God, prepared as a bride adorned for her husband.
> 3. And I heard a loud voice from the throne, saying, "Behold, the tabernacle of God is among the people, and He will dwell among them, and they shall be His people, and God Himself will be among them,"
>
> **Revelation 21:1-3**

Here we see that God's kingdom has been established on earth. A new Jerusalem has been set as the place in Israel from which God will govern the nations of the world. And God will dwell there. The foundations of the new city and the twelve gates of this city establishes the fact that the nation that was assigned by God to serve as the priests to the world (Israel), will finally be functioning in their divine assignment. But what about the other nations? We are told that at this time, there will be no temple, nor will there be a need for the sun and the moon because God will be dwelling in His earthly kingdom and the other nations will be walking in the light that is being provided by God dwelling on earth with men. Note here, the divinely inspired scripture states that the "**nations**" shall walk in the light of God! So how important are the nations and national ethnicities? In a word, VERY!

> *"22. I saw no temple in it, for the Lord God the Almighty and the Lamb are its temple.*
> *23. And the city has no need of the sun or of the moon to shine on it, for the glory of God has illuminated it, and its lamp is the Lamb.*
> *24. The nations will walk by its light, and the kings of the earth will bring their glory into it."*
> **Revelation 21:22-24**

When the scripture says that "the nations will walk by its light", it is saying that the nations will be fulfilling their divine assignments within God's kingdom on earth, just like the angels and orders of angels fulfill their divine assignment in God's kingdom in heaven! And what a glorious time this will be! God is all about order. He did not say that the people will walk by the light, but rather He says the nations will walk by the light. God further emphasizes this by saying that the leaders of the nations (kings) will bring their glory into the kingdom's capital. Every time I read this I think of all of the riches that Queen Makeda brought to Jerusalem when she came to see Solomon. Surely she brought her glory into Jerusalem.

So understanding the biblical nations and ethnic nationalities should be important to you because of the importance that God has placed on it. This is the way in which God has purposed to establish His kingdom on earth. We see at the very beginning God established the nations, He then strategically placed them geographically for their kingdom assignments. He then deeded to each nation the resources needed to fulfill their divine assignment. And in the end, we see that each nation will be fulfilling their assignment in loyalty to the king. Oh what a day!

In closing, I will, for transparency, say that I used to get a little sad when reading this. I worked as a Global technical Manager in my career, and as such I lead a global team and had regular interactions with people from the four corners of the world. All of the people that I interacted with daily knew their country of ethnic origin. I only knew my continent of origin. When they said that they were of Italian ancestry, I could only say that I was of 'African' ancestry. When they said that they were of Finnish ancestry, I still could only say that I was of 'African Ancestry'. When they said that they were of Argentinean ancestry, I could only say that I was of 'African ancestry'. Africa is a huge continent and the current home of numerous countries. But understanding the Bible and searching back through world history, I now know that Sub-Saharan Africa was known as Ethiopia up through the seventeenth century, so today I know that I am of biblical Ethiopian ancestry, and God's word and the World History are in agreement on this. And today I am overfilled with pride just knowing how God used my Ethiopian ancestors to start civilization, develop humanity, and protect righteousness. As black people of the world today, we should live with the understanding of the immense responsibility God has assigned to us in His kingdom on earth. And this should be a immovable part of the Black History that we ensure our future generations of successors know, understand, and hold as a prominent part of their existence.

NOTES

NOTES